Ricky Megee has settle... drawn in early 2008, with his wife, Kate. No longer the guy who survived seventy-one days eating frogs and lizards, Rick is managing a construction team on one of the world's new industrial frontiers. While still surviving in the desert of sorts, Rick is enjoying the opportunity to be recognised for what he does and not who he is.

Greg McLean literally fell into journalism twelve years ago. Since then his career has taken him from Turkey to Tasmania and many interesting places in between. He now lives in Darwin with his partner, Bec, and spends his days mucking around with film and television projects, cheering on the mighty St George Dragons and enjoying a quiet beer with friends and strangers.

LEFT for DEAD

How I survived 71 days in the outback

Ricky Megee

with Greg McLean

ARENA

ALLEN&UNWIN

*Note: This is a true story, however,
some names of people have been changed.*

This edition published in 2010

First published in 2008

Arena, an imprint of
Allen & Unwin
83 Alexander Street
Crows Nest NSW 2065
Australia
Phone: (61 2) 8425 0100
Fax: (61 2) 9906 2218
Email: info@allenandunwin.com
Web: www.allenandunwin.com

Cataloguing-in-Publication details are available
from the National Library of Australia
www.librariesaustralia.nla.gov.au

ISBN 978 1 74237 277 8

Set in 13/16 pt Adobe Garamond Pro by Bookhouse, Sydney
Printed in Australia by McPherson's Printing Group

10 9 8 7 6 5 4 3 2 1

Look the stars for guidance,
Look the stars for light,
Look the stars in times of need,
Their calm will make it right.

Gary Ronald McLean (1971–1994)

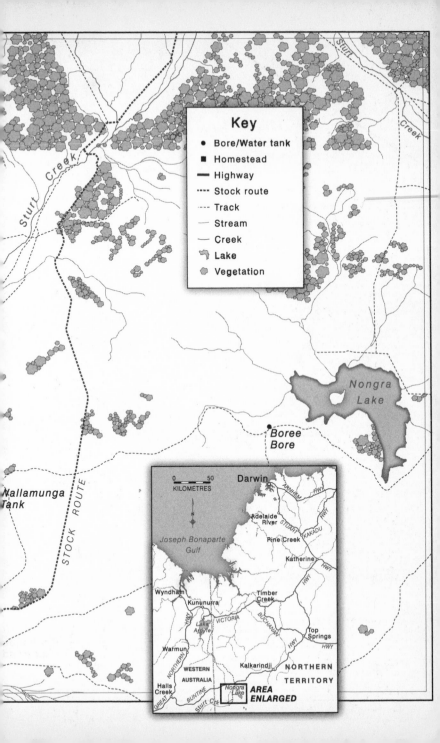

Key

- ● Bore/Water tank
- ■ Homestead
- ▬ Highway
- ┅ Stock route
- ┄ Track
- ── Stream
- ── Creek
- 🏞 Lake
- ⬡ Vegetation

Sturt Creek

Sturt Creek

Nongra Lake

● *Boree Bore*

Nallamunga Tank

STOCK ROUTE

0   50
KILOMETRES

Darwin

Joseph Bonaparte Gulf

Adelaide River

ARNHEM HWY

STUART HWY

KAKADU

Pine Creek

Katherine

Wyndham

Kununurra

Timber Creek

VICTORIA

BUCHANAN

HWY

Lake Argyle

Top Springs

HWY

Warmun

WESTERN AUSTRALIA

Kalkarindji

NORTHERN TERRITORY

NORTHERN

HWY

Halls Creek

GREAT

BUNTINE

Sturt Cr

Nongra Lake **AREA ENLARGED**

INTRODUCTION
By Greg McLean

I first met Ricky Megee in early April 2006, in my role as a journalist for the *Northern Territory News*. His first words to me were along the lines of 'You're the last arsehole I'd talk to'.

Earlier that day the newspaper I worked for had published on its front page the first exclusive article about this mystery man who had been found in the desert. Questions were being asked about who he was and how he had survived for so long under such harsh conditions.

My friend and colleague, Emma Gumbleton, did a really good job in picking up the original story at a Cattlemen's Association conference, but neither the police nor the health department, the two authorities that should have been able to substantiate Rick's survival, could provide any identifying details about him. There were mixed messages being sent through official channels that clouded the picture.

But one thing was for sure—whoever this guy was, he'd done something pretty spectacular.

Our editors sat on it for a few days, trying to get information confirmed, and then they chose to run the story because it was so incredible. A guy living in a humpy for months, eating frogs and lizards, is a story bound to burn a hole in the pocket of even the most patient of newsroom bosses, no matter how difficult it is to verify.

Rick had agreed to talk to us on the morning our first article was published, but then he changed his mind after taking offence at a few things in the original story. The headline announced, 'Mystery Man Survives Three Months Lost in Desert'. When I first talked to him on the phone, I let him vent his anger over being labelled a mystery man, explained how our story had been researched and verified, and left it at that. A couple of days later I called him again and he agreed to meet me for lunch at a local café.

He wasn't hard to identify sitting outside the Fannie Bay Cool Spot. There aren't many adult men I meet who are skinnier than me—I'm six-foot-four and weigh less than 70 kilograms, but this guy beat me hands down. With his beard shaved off, he didn't look as old as in the photos I'd seen; but the compression bandages covering his calf muscles gave him away as he sat outside overlooking the oceanic panorama of nearby East Point. A plate of chips and a strawberry milkshake and we were on our way.

Ricky seemed very genuine and we struck up a friendship pretty well immediately, catching up as regularly as we could after that. He didn't say much about it, but I thought he might be doing it pretty hard emotionally during this period. It's not every day someone tries to kill you, and that was only the start of it for him. Physically, in those first few weeks,

I could see his ankles were far from all right and watched on as he underwent the saga of an unsuccessful operation.

Above all, I found him to be a really decent bloke who was in a jam and I offered to help him out in any way I could.

He's certainly never had a problem with his appetite since I've known him. It was phenomenal to watch him pile on the kilos every week. We ended up living together for six months and formed a friendship based on trust and respect that I'm sure will endure longer than most.

In working with him on this book, but more importantly as a friend, I've listened for many hours to Rick's accounts of what happened in the desert. My conclusion is he's one tough bastard. He would never take a backward step from any challenge.

Now that I know him so well, it comes as no surprise to realise that Ricky Megee survived what no other Westerner has since Australia's desert interior was first penetrated by our nation's white pioneers almost 200 years ago. Except they had horses, donkeys, camels, Aboriginal trackers, Afghan cameleers, provisions, a map, compass, water—all the help you rely on for an expedition into some of the most inhospitable territory on the planet.

What Rick lived through is nothing short of horrific. He is one of the first people I'd choose to have standing by my side if I was facing danger. Not because he survived 71 days in the desert but because that's the type of bloke he is. A friend of the first order, who sticks to his guns regardless of the adversity.

I hope you appreciate his remarkable story.

PROLOGUE

I was lying in a hole. Under something. A tarp, maybe. It was a dugout. Like a shallow grave that hadn't been filled in yet. My grave. I'd been dumped alive in a hole and left for dead.

Something was spread over my face. Sand. I wiggled my toes. No shoes. I struggled to move, felt my pockets for my lighter. Nothing. Cigarettes—gone.

Where was I? I had no clue. Something was pushing through the tarp. The sound of sniffing. Dogs, maybe.

I wriggled and pushed myself up, forcing back the cover. Into daylight. And heat. Now I was face to face with a pack of dogs. Dingoes, ready to sit down to dinner.

I pushed my way out of the hole, shooing the dingoes away in the process. They didn't go quietly, growling viciously as they retreated. I aimed a few rocks at the sniffing bastards to scatter them. I wasn't exactly a small bloke, tipping the scales at 105 kilograms, with a hulking physique that was more muscle than fat. I felt more than capable of wrestling a pack of wild dingoes if it came down to that.

With the dingoes sorted, I looked around. I was in the middle of nowhere. Nothing but dirt, rocks, the odd clump of grass and a few scattered trees. No sign of where I came from and no one to share my growing misery with.

Bloody stony country. Where are my shoes? I turned back to look inside the hole I'd crawled out of and sifted through the sand, but there was no sign of my boots. They were long gone.

How the hell had I ended up with rocks and dingoes and not much else for company? I knew I had to find a way out quick smart. But it only took me my first few steps over the pin-sharp contours of the rocky outcrop that surrounded me for it to really sink in. With no boots, I was in a bad way. The jagged edges hidden beneath the sandy surface dug into my tender soles. The pain was crippling, magnified by the trauma of having to bear my full weight on my mangled right ankle. I'd badly injured it in a work accident and now here I was walking without a leg brace for the first time in two years.

It struck me that I had a vehicle somewhere. I definitely had wheels when I'd started this trip. But the car was nowhere to be seen either.

No shoes, no vehicle, no food, no water and no idea. I'd always been one of those blokes ragging on people who found themselves lost in the desert, putting shit on them for being so stupid. Now I was one of those people.

It was harsh, desolate country for a man all alone in bare feet. Tough country. But I started to walk. And walk. The more I walked, I figured, the less distance I'd have to travel to get found.

It was faulty logic, but it was the best I could come up with.

1

RICKY JOHN MEGEE

I was born Ricky John Megee at Leongatha Hospital on 4 June 1970. My parents, Wendy and Peter, had a dairy farm about 50 kilometres out of a small Victorian town in the Gippsland region. This is where I spent my first five years living in a kid's paradise with my younger sisters, Tracey, Tina and Vicki, usually trailing close behind.

In those very early years I was my dad's shadow, helping him milk the cows, going with him for a ride on the motorbike around the paddocks or hunting for rabbits in the hills until all hours. I loved the farm and I loved my dad and he loved me.

He was an angry little bloke of Irish descent not much more than five foot tall—a hard man, a short man, and I wanted to be just like him. People who knew him would say he had a big chip on little shoulders which I inherited. Except for my height—I'm over six foot—which is a legacy from my mother.

The son of a strict Catholic family, my dad met Mum when she was just seventeen. He soon won her heart with his charming sense of humour and commitment, and before too long they were happily married and planning a family of their own.

They had a loving relationship in those days, apparently. But they both began to tire of the hours required to make a go of the farm. Before I even reached kindergarten they sold up, with plans to return to Melbourne and live an easier life in the suburbs.

Dad landed a job with the gas company CIG and we moved into a three-bedroom flat in the outer suburb of Sunshine, a place not at all like it sounds. Because Dad was doing shiftwork, he began spending a lot of time at the pub afterwards to have some kind of social interaction.

That was when he hit his bad patch. The more he drank, the more frustrated Mum became by his behaviour, and the arguments grew more heated and more frequent.

After about a year of the drinking and fighting, Mum had had enough and packed us kids up and moved out to a nearby suburb. Dad took the break-up real hard and sank even further into the black hole that had consumed him in a wash of grog and despair. He still saw us kids when he could arrange it and was especially close to me, but he seemed lost without his family.

About six months after we moved out I came home from school one day and Mum told me that Dad had died in a car accident. I was gobsmacked; I didn't really know what to say or how to react. What could I say—my dad was my hero and now all of a sudden Mum was telling me he was dead.

I largely kept my shattered feelings to myself, carrying on as normally as possible to protect my family from dealing with my sadness when they needed me most. It wasn't until the following weekend, when we went up to Mum's parents' place at Sunshine, that I learned what really happened.

My grandparents liked a drink but didn't really seem to get on with each other, unless they were both throwing insults blind rotten drunk. In their happier drunk moments, one of them might smash a pool cue over the other one's head. This would be followed up with a healthy dose of verbal abuse that continued until the ambulance arrived. It could be that kind of place.

But while my grandparents were volatile towards each other, they were harmless when it came to us grandkids. They still fussed over us and made us feel welcome, they just weren't very good at playing the doting grandparents because they struggled so hard at keeping themselves sober.

That weekend I was helping my grandma prepare a Sunday roast when she blurted out that my dad didn't die in a car accident. The banging plates and dropped pots suggested she'd had a few drinks already, but she told me straight-faced that Dad had shot himself.

Her admission came as a big blow, and I didn't know whether to believe her or not. She was clearly pissed and had always ragged on my dad, so it might just have been another lie he couldn't defend. But I told Mum what was said and she confirmed it was the truth.

For the rest of the day Mum and my grandma screamed tirelessly at each other; Mum was fuming and my grandma was always up for a good slanging match, so it was bound to go on for a few hours. As I'd assumed the role of the man of the house already, my first priority was to make sure my little sisters were out of earshot and away from all the mudslinging.

Having that responsibility at such a young age was something I took very seriously, especially with Mum having to do shiftwork as a factory machinist to put food on the table for all of us. Although only seven years old, I held up my end of the arrangement by making the girls' lunches and getting them off to school in clean clothes each day.

I also picked up a paper run before school that earned the family another $24 a week. To add to the tally, I used to pinch the odd loaf of bread or carton of milk from people's doorsteps—never enough to leave a family short at the breakfast table, just a bit extra to help feed mine. Sometimes I'd pocket little cakes from the corner store for my sisters' playlunch when the shopkeeper wasn't looking so Mum didn't have to worry about it, but I'd hardly call that thieving.

School was all right in the first few years—I breezed through primary without having to put in too much effort, but by the time I hit high school I felt like I was twelve going on twenty and didn't enjoy that bossy environment anymore. Outside of school my world revolved around adults—they were who I talked to and related to and I was mostly treated like one myself.

I was also no longer prepared to tolerate fools. Being at the bottom of the food chain again meant that all of a sudden it wasn't just teachers telling me what to do, but other, older kids who thought they were that much bigger and tougher than me. They'd soon learn otherwise.

Dealing with the men in Mum's life had become another headache entirely. Mum started dating again about six months after Dad died—I think she missed the companionship and wanted some stability in her life. It was a whole new experience for her as my dad had been the first and only man in her life up until then, so she didn't really know where to begin on the singles scene.

Most of the blokes she brought home couldn't handle me; I thought they were trying to muscle in on our family and made it as uncomfortable as possible for them. I considered myself the man of the house and didn't take too kindly to strangers trying to impose themselves on us.

A few came and went, but eventually Mum met Jim. She was introduced to him at a social function she attended with another guy. Her date ended up being good friends with Jim, who wasted no time turning up the heat on my mum. He did his mate out of a girlfriend and cemented himself in our lives in one fell swoop.

Mum was pretty naive when it came to men and what they wanted from her. I think she was looking to fill that nurturing void in her life when Jim appeared on the scene with all his charm and swagger. He was all right to us kids in the beginning and bought a house in the neighbourhood we all shared. But before too long his true colours came shining through.

Besides constantly making demands on Mum—ordering her about like she was the maid—he came with a set of annoying house rules. Rules such as what time us kids had to be in bed and how he expected us to treat him didn't take into account the fact that we'd managed quite well on our own for two years before he turned up.

In the circumstances I made it pretty easy for him for the next three years, putting up with his insults without retaliating. But finally his physical assaults pushed me over the edge. I just snapped one day when he was having a go at me. Reaching for the kitchen drawer on impulse, I pulled out a knife and pushed it towards him.

As I stared daggers at him, Jim knew that while I was only thirteen, I'd go through with it if he didn't pull his head in. By now Mum was frantically trying to calm us both down but it wasn't much use, I was going off my nut.

Jim backed down, and I put the knife back in the kitchen drawer. But not before giving him a few solemn words of advice. If he ever touched me or my family again, I'd stab him while he was asleep.

After that it was a case of either he went or I did. So Mum packed up our bags and we left Jim; we moved to the outer Melbourne suburb of Dandenong.

Once the turmoil with Jim had settled down, Mum started going out to the pub again for an occasional drink and a giggle with her girlfriends, which is how she met her second husband, Rob. They seemed to hit it off almost immediately, enabling him to quietly slip into our lives under the guise of a shining knight in protective armour.

Rob was a tradesman who had custody of two kids of his own about our age; at first he appeared to be a good influence on the family. As is often the case though, you can't judge a book by its cover. This especially applied to Rob, as the cover looked good but the book was full of shit.

When he started coming around home all us kids thought he was pretty cool; he seemed to enjoy mucking around with us and made it clear he didn't want to play the role of our dad. Quite often he'd take us all out to the pub for a counter meal, letting us order whatever we wanted and sneaking us in to have a game on the pokies when the barman wasn't looking. When things became more serious between him and Mum, they found a house we could all live in. We were the modern-day Brady Bunch—six young kids with different parents all living under the one roof.

As well as changing address I joined a new high school up the road, the Dandenong North Technical College for Boys. It was one of those rough all-boys schools where you needed a timetable to work out which fights you wanted to watch during the lunch break, like a fight club training ground for adolescents.

I was a pretty placid sort of kid normally and wasn't into fighting much, but you didn't get a choice at this place. My reluctance to join in the brawling made me a prime target for regular beatings, but it wasn't anything I couldn't handle.

On the home front Rob was fraying at the edges as the burden of being a closet alcoholic brought him undone. We wouldn't learn about his alcoholism until years later, but it transformed him into an unpleasant person to have around.

No one really thought much about the fact he had a few beers at home after work every day—after all, everyone's entitled to a few beers after work. But, as his workmates would later reveal to our family, those few beers at home were on top of the six to ten he'd already consumed on the company clock.

Because Rob worked for a big utilities company and was good at his job he could do enough in the first few hours to keep the boss happy. Then he'd spend the rest of the working day getting plastered, without anyone caring too much about where he was. It certainly explained why he was always so chirpy when he arrived home from work. He looked happy to have been sweating it out all day, keen to sink his teeth into a cold beer.

Around this time I was enrolled at Syndal High School, another unhappy arrangement for everyone involved. Once again I stuck out in the playground like a sore thumb. Pretty quickly the alpha males singled me out for refusing to join the cool kids in their bullying ways.

The three kids who supposedly ran the tough element of the class didn't appreciate my rejection of them and their shallow displays of intimidation. In retaliation my three tormentors were forever hassling me, calling me names or pushing me around a little when they had strength in numbers. But it all came to a shuddering halt in home economics class one afternoon, when one of the toughs persisted in flicking me with a tea-towel.

I told him several times there would be trouble if he kept going, but he ignored me. After warning him one final time, I promptly pulled a big knife from the drawer and swung around with just enough venom for him to think I would do a lot more than simply threaten him with it.

'Don't fuck with me, buddy!' It was a very simple message, but one I delivered with the utmost sincerity.

This show of resistance earned me an eight-week suspension, which didn't really bother me. It was a shitty school anyway. From then on I vowed to get in first if ever I felt threatened—I'd never take shit from anyone; I'd throw the first punch and not stop swinging until everyone else had.

Mum and Rob were happily married and the news of my latest indiscretion didn't go down so well around the kitchen table. They were worried I was becoming uncontrollable and decided a permanent change of scenery might help settle me down, whether I liked it or not.

Rob had a block of land out in the country at St Arnaud which they thought could be the tonic, so we packed up and moved our Brady Bunch out of the suburbs. St Arnaud was a decent enough town and I managed to scrape through Year 10 without pulling a knife on anyone.

Although I really wanted to become a pilot, it felt more urgent to join the workforce and finally gain my own independence. To achieve this, I left school and picked up a job with an electrician Rob knew in the area.

I didn't really like the electrical trade but I stuck it out in St Arnaud for a few years before moving to Adelaide, which was completely foreign to me. I didn't know anyone and that was part of the attraction.

Finding work was easy enough, but the city itself didn't gel with me and after six months I packed up again and moved to Gympie in Queensland. I landed a job at the local timber mill there, where the money was good. I was also able to get my tickets, allowing me to operate the different types of heavy machinery there, and that made it worthwhile.

The town itself was full of blokes whose greatest aim in life was to get pissed at the pub and try and root anything that moved. A funny place to meet your wife, but this was the case for me with Alison.

2

LOST LOVE

I met Alison at the pub in Gympie and managed to snap her up pretty easily. Most of the other guys in town were boofheads so she appreciated a guy actually talking to her.

Alison was very attractive and what you'd call a bloke's girl. The kind of woman who would stand up and piss next to you in the trough just for a laugh. She was a lot of fun most of the time and physically stunning, but also a handful.

Her parents were very well-off, so all she had to worry about was her next hair appointment. That scenario soon grew tiresome for both of us and to escape the fishbowl of her home town we moved to Brisbane, where I landed a job as an assistant warehouse manager.

She was a bit hard to handle in the big city after never having to work a day in her life. I'm sure that was part of the reason her parents were glad for me to take her off their hands.

We partied hard for the first year or so in Brisbane. I was making enough money to buy us a new car, and to put a deposit on a three-bedroom brick veneer house in Springwood to complete the picture.

Alison was starting to talk about having kids, so with this in mind I took on a new job as a carpet salesman for the extra money offered.

Who would've ever thought I'd make it as a carpet salesman? They were throwing the cash at me by the square metre. Before too long I was managing two stores, putting in 80-hour working weeks to get us ahead. Alison even found a part-time job for the first time in her life, to put some extra dollars in the bank.

After almost three years together, we got married and seemed to have a comfortable future ahead of us. But within three months of walking down the aisle we split. It just didn't work out.

I moved to Townsville in north Queensland on my own and got a job on a prawn trawler. I spent a couple of seasons out at sea working as a deckhand, and it was one of the most trouble-free periods of my life. The work was hard, but there is nothing else to do out on a prawn boat except to slave away and then go to sleep. You just roll up your sleeves and get on with it. Whenever I returned to shore, I would get into the piss and smoke pot without a worry in the world. It was a simple life that caused no harm to anyone.

Eighteen months later I returned to Brisbane with enough money saved up to start my own landscaping business. I was soon earning a living, but managing a business ended up being more of a commitment than I was prepared to give at that time. The satisfaction of owning my own business was soon overshadowed by the attraction of a bigger pay packet for regular hours.

I decided to get rid of the landscaping business and go back to sales jobs for the easy money and convenience. To pick up some extra cash on the side, I did security work in clubs at nights.

Once again the money was good, but being a bouncer didn't really agree with me. The meatheads who dominated the industry were a bit much to cope with. But it gave me a good insight into how the nightclub industry operated, and who the major players were.

Through introductions and word of mouth, I met a couple of guys who ran the Valley nightclub district. Soon enough I picked up work from them as a freelance debt collector. I was big and strong and took shit from no one.

That job worked well for me and, in the two years I chased up their debts, I never once missed out on a collect. While I never killed or maimed anyone, there were certain measures that had to be taken. Anyone who had to cough up knew the consequences were severe if they didn't do the right thing.

I only ever used any form of violence as a last resort and it was rare for it to come to that. There are other methods to get what you want from people, ones that don't involve your fists. If that meant grabbing the keys of a new BMW and driving off in it to settle a debt, then that was how it was. If they wanted to stop me, they only had to say so; if not, then the debt was paid. I was very good at my job and that earned me a name in certain circles.

My effectiveness as a freelancer didn't sit too well with the bikies who used to do the debt collecting for this particular group. The cops had also cottoned on to who I was and kept pretty close tabs on me because of the people I worked for. But they could never pin me for anything because 99 per cent of the time I wasn't doing anything wrong.

One day in the late 1990s one of the feds pulled me aside in a suburban McDonald's car park, and gave me the option of coming to work for them to infiltrate some of the organisations I worked for, otherwise I would end up dead or in jail. I chose Option D, which was to go straight home and pack my bags. I knew it was time to leave town quietly, and without question. My then girlfriend, Petra, didn't hesitate in joining me and we were on the next plane as swift as an avalanche—to Perth, about as far away from Brisbane as I could think of and no looking back.

We'd been in Perth for about five weeks when our plan for a peaceful existence turned pear-shaped, all because of a stupid mistake of mine. I'd been at home for most of the day, drinking scotch, when a mate who lived locally but who I knew from Queensland called me up wanting a ride into town.

I told him I was too pissed to drive, but to come over for a drink anyway. After a few more Scotches, he convinced me to drive him in to meet another guy for a night on the town with the boys. Just like the old days, he reckoned. With that much Scotch in me, I didn't need my arm twisted very far.

The three of us hit the nightclubs in the city but got rejected from most of them because my mate only had runners on. As we were walking through the park, feeling a bit dejected from our half-arsed night, we were approached by six deadshits my mate's mate had had a prior run-in with.

They made it pretty clear they were going to belt us up, for the simple fact we were with this other guy. Simple as that. But me and my mate had other ideas and chopped into four of them in a matter of seconds. Then we chased the other two down as they ran across the park and gave them what-for as well.

The guy the fight was over ended up without a scratch on him and me and my mate felt all right, so we decided to try a few more clubs before calling it a night. Stupidly, my mate grabbed a pair of shoes from one of the bashed blokes so he could get into the nightclubs easier, and that's where our trouble started.

As we made our way back into town, a patrol car picked up the two guys we had chased down on the riverbank. They told them that we'd beaten the six of them up in an unprovoked attack and stolen their shoes.

The next thing we knew, the sirens were wailing from all directions and me and my mate were cornered and thrown into jail, charged with robbery with violence. It didn't matter to the cops that the six people we beat up actually started the fight, or that it was one pair of shoes we pinched from them.

After four months on remand, I was sentenced to a maximum of three years jail with eight months minimum to serve in maximum security at Casuarina prison.

Jail wasn't that bad—I got a job as a cook so there was always plenty of food around, which was my main priority. I kept out of trouble because I could get on well with all the competing groups inside. If there were ever any issues to deal with, I could look after myself well enough.

I actually had the pleasure of spending an extra week in jail because, seven days short of completing my sentence, the parole board informed me that, due to the nature of my charge, I had to complete a two-week anger management course before I could be released. Apparently, they'd forgotten to enrol me before my parole date. It was great news to hear before heading off to an anger management course!

Due to a contact I met in jail, as a free man I landed a job working as a gardener at the casino. I don't know if it was because of the time I had spent locked up or not, but slowly Petra became more of a best friend than a girlfriend to me. I loved her deeply but there was no longer a spark between us, and I could see no hope of me being the one to re-ignite it.

That's what made it so hard when I met Misha out at a club in Perth one night and we fell madly in love with each other; the electricity between us outweighed any negatives. We connected on just about every level and moved in together almost as soon as we met, happy and completely in love.

But I couldn't shake the feeling karma was about to catch up with me. Right on cue, I fucked up again when I ran into some old connections who asked me to do a couple of debt collecting jobs for them around town. I thought that would be fine—a bit of pocket money cleaning up a few jobs for the boys. But soon enough these odd jobs became my main source of income and my courier business became the odd job.

Although I wasn't caught doing anything illegal, I again came to the attention of the local police. I realised the heat was rising and, to get out of the kitchen, I convinced Misha to move to Sydney with me; to start afresh without the temptation of collecting debts hovering over us.

We landed on our feet almost immediately when I picked up a job operating excavators; we found a nice place of our own near the water at Rose Bay. Our neighbourhood was one of those stuffy suburbs filled with old money, but it was close to the city and the beach and a few shops.

Sadly, Sydney didn't gel with Misha and its attractions weren't as strong as the pull of her family. She moved back home to Perth after a few months, a sad but predictable end to our impulsive love affair.

For me, the decision to remain in Sydney was about making money while enjoying the good life a big city offers. With this in mind, I started up my own home improvements business around 2002; I employed a licensed builder and a few labourers with the aim of targeting the smaller jobs that paid better.

Instead of spending four or five months building a house, we concentrated on constructing patios and pergolas and sheds and decks that could be done for a greater profit margin. We also took on the dangerous jobs, like erecting balconies over cliff faces, which other builders would put in the too-hard basket; the rewards were handsome.

After two years this business was making buckets of money and I was relishing the challenge of going to work every day. Then one morning it all turned to shit in a split second. Swinging over the edge of a cliff at one of those big plush properties overlooking Sydney's northern beaches, while building a fancy patio, I somehow slipped and fell 7 metres onto the rocks below. The shuddering impact of landing on my feet left me sprawled on the rocks, with my tibia and fibula bones snapped in half and two broken ankles.

The terrain prevented paramedics from accessing the accident site from the ground and they had to call in a rescue chopper to winch me to safety. All I hoped for was that they had a good supply of painkillers.

What followed was twelve months in and out of hospitals in a bid to avoid the amputation of my right foot, among other medical adventures. I spent the first three weeks in St George Hospital dosed up on drugs, as my ankles were still too swollen for surgeons to operate. Finally the swelling went down and they put me under the knife, inserting enough steel in my legs during the operations to manufacture a small car.

Another two and a half months in rehabilitation followed before I could check myself out of hospital, with two broken ankles in plaster. I couldn't really do anything for myself around the house; I was virtually incapacitated. After a couple of frustrating weeks fumbling to look after myself, I accepted an offer from my sister, Tina, to fly to Brisbane and recover at her place.

Soon after I arrived in Brisbane, I went to hospital for a check-up, to sort out why there was pus oozing from my ankle like lava from an erupting volcano. The doctor there took one look at it and wanted to operate within hours, suspecting I'd picked up a staph infection that was eating the bone of my ankle away. They dosed me up with enough painkillers to knock out an angry rhino. I wouldn't have felt a wrecking ball hit me in the face.

The first exploratory operation to survey the damage showed that a big chunk of my ankle had already turned to mush. The prognosis sounded beyond ordinary. My surgeon's opinion was I had a 90 per cent chance of losing my foot and he wanted me to sign a consent form allowing him to amputate if he deemed it necessary.

I couldn't believe what I was hearing. After going to hospital for what I thought was a routine check-up on my progress, I was now being asked for permission to chop my foot off to cover someone else's incompetence. I told the surgeon in no uncertain terms that under no circumstances would I ever consent to him or anyone else amputating my foot. The only way to achieve that was over my dead body. As far as I was concerned, my life was over if I lost my foot and I wasn't going to simply roll over and let that happen for any old reason.

The only other option, he explained, was to undergo an operation every second day for sixteen days. That way the surgeons could slowly blast away the infected bone and pull out the dead bits of meat while flushing out the joints.

It was considered an extremely risky procedure as most people can't handle going under full anaesthetic so regularly. Different people react differently and in the absolute worst case the consequences could kill me.

For me it was a no-brainer, so I told them to get to work. They could saw into me with all the surgical tools in their kit bag if it meant my foot stayed intact.

Drifting in and out of consciousness for the next two weeks, in between the procession of scalpels, the pain felt savage but my resolve to see the procedure through never wavered. The doctors were amazed my body could tolerate such constant high doses of anaesthetic and still be responsive on the ward when they required. But in my eyes that had to be my attitude. How else was I to respond?

When the doc sucked out the last of the previous hospital's poison, to signal the beginning of my next round of reconstructive surgery, he left behind a hole measuring 15 centimetres by 8 centimetres where my ankle used to be. To repair the damage, surgeons had to cut a length of muscle from my groin about 25 centimetres long to pack into the side of my foot. They then took a skin graft off my other thigh to attach it all together.

The surgeon told me there was still a good chance his prolonged experiment wouldn't work and they'd have to amputate my foot anyway. Even if the muscle did manage to fuse there was no way I'd regain any use of my ankle, the doc reassured me. It was all just cosmetic improvement.

Full of nothing but bad news he was; I used his words as inspiration. By the time they'd finished having their wicked way with me, I'd been in their hospital for another ten weeks of my life. I had virtually no visitors for most of that time. Anyone who wanted to see me had to put on a kind of space suit to enter the isolation ward, in case I picked up another infection. Like the bubble boy, I needed to be careful not to catch anyone else's germs.

I also possessed a tolerance to incredible pain due to the dosages of painkillers I didn't like being familiar with—pumped full of enough to feel constantly numb. When it was time to finally leave hospital, the doctors piled me up with so many boxes of painkillers it looked like I'd robbed the chemist on the way out.

With eight to ten pills to digest with every meal, I felt like my own nurse. I had to separate the different colours and make sure I took them in the correct dosages, or else I'd be sick or in shocking pain. After several months though I was able to slowly wean myself off the painkillers and begin rehabilitation.

My sister, Tina, is the one who really took care of me, though. Not since we were kids had we been that close or reliant on each other. Because I was in a wheelchair, with both my legs still in plaster due to the surgery, she became my life support while I recuperated. She was my legs and the person who provided me with almost all my daily needs as a disabled person.

The damage caused by the infection and subsequent surgery meant I had to virtually learn how to walk all over again. My ankle didn't exist anymore, more or less, because the infection had eaten most of the bone and muscle away. But with nothing better to do, I put every effort into my recovery. I constantly exercised my ankle, regardless of any pain, to stimulate muscle growth.

Eventually the docs measured me up for an external fixator, which bolted onto my left leg to keep everything in place, and I graduated from a wheelchair to crutches. After two months with the bolt-on attached to my leg, they gave me a split cast, meaning I could walk on my mangled foot at last.

My progress astonished the doctors. They had expected me to lose the use of my foot entirely, but instead I came close to getting back full use of it in a matter of months.

The leg brace would have to stay attached for a couple of years, but my foot was saved.

I decided to remain in Brisbane, once the doctors gave me the all clear. I moved out of Tina's to give her back her own space and found a place of my own. I landed a job as operations manager for a company selling containment systems for problem pets. I felt good about getting my life back on track in Brisbane.

Throughout my ordeal in hospital I stayed in touch with Julie. She was a Canadian nurse who had treated me at St George Hospital in Sydney, where I originally caught the infection. I thought she was really cute from the moment I saw her on the ward. We openly flirted with each other when I wasn't knocked out on painkillers.

Spending so much time alone in hospital up in Brisbane made me think of her even more. When I could manage to take care of myself again, I rang her and told her I wanted to be with her. She felt the same about me and threw in her job to come and live in Brisbane so we could be together for three months, until her working visa expired.

When the day arrived for her to board the plane back to Canada, I promised her I would be over there as soon as I could arrange it. A few months later I flew to Calgary to be with her on her turf and see if we were really meant to be.

Julie was as perfect as ever, but my fear of commitment led to me stuffing things up again. She started talking about marriage and spending the rest of our lives together; I baulked and scared her off by making up stories of sleeping with other women since I'd been with her.

Back in Brisbane I slipped into security work again and ended up hooking up with this crazy bitch, Sarah. She and I were at each other's throat throughout our brief but stormy relationship, until finally declaring we hated each other.

She moved to Port Hedland in Western Australia to clear her head and I was left in Brisbane scratching mine. I was sick to death of the whole security scene I'd returned to and the partying that had become the focus of my life again. At 35 years old I was stuck in a rut and I wanted a change.

Then Sarah rang up out of the blue and told me she'd got it together and had a good job in Port Hedland. She said there was plenty of work and wanted us to try again. I didn't think twice about jumping in the car and driving across the country to see for myself.

3

TAKING THE BAIT

It wasn't as if I really expected to get back with Sarah. She sounded reasonable enough on the phone, and in between all the fighting and arguing we did have some fun together, but it was clear we weren't going to spend the rest of our lives with each other.

Still, her suggestion to come and check out Port Hedland gave me an excuse to get out of Brisbane once and for all. Away from the temptations and old friends that were bound to bring me undone. It didn't take long to pack up my life because there wasn't that much to stay for, I just had to store some furniture at a mate's place and pack my bags.

I'd recently bought a late model Mitsubishi Challenger four-wheel drive from some people I knew through acquaintances selling it cheap. I stocked it up with the bare necessities required to start a clean slate on the other side of the country—clothes, tools, food, water and an Esky. I had

5000 kilometres of uninspiring road in front of me and not a worry in the world. Anyone who sees beauty in monotonous flat dirt as far as the eye can see is a better man than me.

The quicker the blandness of outback Queensland bled into the plain emptiness of the Northern Territory, the faster my new life would begin. Mount Isa, Longreach, Camooweal, Elliott, Three Ways, Top Springs, Kalkaringi. The landscape across the interior changed gradually from place to place, but over the thousands of kilometres, the transformation was hardly recognisable.

The Territory's unlimited highways crystallised in me the realisation I was entering the unknown—a new environment, new people, a new experience. I crossed into Western Australia with a calm sense of excitement about moving to Port Hedland, arriving at the border enthusiastic about living in a sleepy mining town where just about everyone came from somewhere else.

On the way to my potential new home in the Pilbara, I stopped in at Halls Creek, just across the West Australian border, to look up an old friend. After I tracked him down at his home, my mate explained over a few beers that his teenage son needed to get to Adelaide later that month to see some family.

My plans were to keep heading north to Port Hedland, to see what was there for me. But I told him I could maybe take his young fella down south if things worked out all right with Sarah and I found a decent job—and he paid for my petrol and expenses. We left it at that and I jumped back in the car the next morning, ready as ever to knock over the last stretch of highway through the Pilbara.

For the first week or so in Port Hedland I stayed with Sarah, and, to her credit, she had improved as a human. She was much more tolerable than when we were together in Brisbane, but not enough for me to want to live with her permanently.

Port Hedland seemed a decent enough town, though. Considering I didn't have anywhere else in particular to go, I was happy enough to stick around and see what eventuated.

Out of interest one morning, I popped in to the local Centrelink to ask about any jobs in the area. As it happened, the helpful woman behind the counter informed me there was a vacancy going in their office as the Aboriginal liaison and human relations manager. Applications were closing, but the candidates were pretty ordinary apparently and I was welcome to apply.

The job paid over $60,000 and the Port Hedland Centrelink seemed full of delightful women. They were quite taken by a guy walking into the office wearing a nice new suit; since I had my resumé with me, I put my hand up for their gig.

They interviewed me there and then and all but gave me the keys to the office, except they had to wait until the boss came back the following week to give the final tick of approval. I certainly didn't mind the idea of sitting on my arse all day in an air-conditioned office full of women who enjoyed the attention.

Thinking the job was all but stitched up and I had time up my sleeve, I drove back to Halls Creek to see my mate. I offered to take his son down to Adelaide if he still needed a ride.

My mate had just won a building contract and had heaps of work on. I knew I'd be sorted for a job if the Centrelink job fell through, and felt I could do with the break down south if I was going to start working full time up the top end of the country for a while.

The journey to Adelaide was uneventful and I spent a few days with the family of my mate's son's girlfriend, who came from there. I hadn't meant to hang around with them for so long. I just meant to pop my head in to be polite, and then head into the city and book a room in a hotel after dropping the young fella off. But they kept having barbecues and taking me to places where the parties didn't stop and the beers kept flowing. It was hard to refuse.

The big boss back at Centrelink in Port Hedland eventually phoned to say that the job was mine with an immediate start. All I had to do was make it back to Port Hedland within the week, as long as all my references checked out. I soon sobered up and rejoined reality. Thanks for the party, fellas, but destiny calls.

I'd driven up and down the Stuart Highway plenty of times over the years. I enjoyed motoring through the spaciousness of the desert, with nothing but ideas rolling through my head. Charging back up the familiar track, thinking about life, I couldn't help but smile about how well things were turning out for me since deciding to leave Brisbane. A well-paid job in a cushy office full of friendly women, no hang-ups from the past and a positive outlook on the future. For the first time since I'd stuffed things up in Canada, my wayward life seemed to be settling into place. Only a few thousand kilometres of highway separated me from a slice of the easy life.

Because I still had a couple of days up my sleeve before starting my new job, I planned to go via Halls Creek and have another night with my mate. I figured he'd be good for a beer and a bed after the favour I'd done him driving his son to Adelaide. He didn't know I was coming but I knew he'd be at home putting his feet up after a hard day's work.

I turned left off the Stuart Highway near Dunmarra, about 500 kilometres south of Darwin, and hit the dirt of the Buchanan Highway heading towards Top Springs. By taking the short cut I was confident I could make it to Halls Creek before dusk.

The road was not much more than a goat track and had its fair share of potholes. But it saved a couple of hours not sticking to the highway, and there were no annoying caravans to contend with.

Once you reach the petrol station at Top Springs, you can turn left and follow the Buntine Highway for about 600 kilometres to Halls Creek. Alternatively, you can turn right, driving towards the Victoria Highway intersection and heading for Kununurra further north. As I was intending to camp at Halls Creek for the night, I turned left. When I got to the small Aboriginal community of Kalkaringi, about 200 kilometres down the highway, I decided to stop and fuel up for the final leg of the day.

Dusty and decrepit-looking, Kalkaringi is typical of the Aboriginal communities that dot the remote outback. There was a large contingent of locals to be found eating chicken drumsticks outside the local shop cum petrol station. I'd run out of petrol on that exact stretch of dirt in the past, thinking I could get all the way to Halls Creek from Top Springs without stopping. I had no intention of repeating that mistake.

It was just after lunch when I pulled out from the bowser at Kalkaringi and cracked my first can of rum and Coke, which had been cooling in my Esky. On about my third can, rattling along on the rain-corrugated road, I came across three fellow travellers sitting on the side of the supposed highway. They flagged me over next to their broken-down Kingswood. I'd helped out plenty of stranded travellers in the past and had no dramas stopping to see what the problem was.

Not many vehicles travel the Buntine in January because it's mostly dirt and the road can get washed out in the wet season. I knew if I drove past them they'd be waiting in the sun for a while, and the sun's pretty damn hot at that time of year. Still, there were a few precautions I always followed for my own protection when helping out anyone on relatively remote stretches of road. I discovered long ago that preventing a problem beats dealing with it.

I pulled up a safe distance in front of the Kingswood and indicated for one of them to come and explain what they needed. All the doors of my car were locked and the windows wound up except for the front seat passenger side. I had my bases covered if he did try and jump in without an invite.

If more than one person approached the vehicle after I told them otherwise, I'd drive off and not look back. There would be no opportunity to punch me or pull out a weapon if I hit the accelerator. I also carried a machete under the driver's seat, just in case things ever turned nasty.

The guy who approached me was aged in his late twenties and looked innocent enough. He explained they'd run out of fuel and he needed a lift to Halls Creek. In hindsight I should've clicked that he didn't ask me if I had any spare fuel first, or questioned why he wasn't trying to get to Kalkaringi, which was much closer in the opposite direction. But my mind was floating elsewhere and I indicated for him to get in.

I watched him in the rear-vision mirror as he ran back to tell his two mates sweltering against their car that he'd hitched a ride with me to Halls Creek. The bossiest one in the group, who looked like he was in his mid to late thirties, gave my passenger some last-minute instructions. A younger quiet guy, probably in his early twenties, stood alongside them, listening passively.

I unlocked the door for my eager hitchhiker, pleased I could do someone a favour in the circumstances. Being from a remote community—where English is a second, third or fifth language—he didn't talk much. It was not until I indicated for him to grab a cold can out of the Esky at his feet and have a drink that he became more animated.

The rum loosened his lips a little, but neither of us could really be that bothered to understand the other beyond the polite basics. There was no need to make irrelevant small talk. We were just two blokes going in the same direction, only one had petrol and one didn't.

About twenty minutes into our silent glide across the top edge of the Western Desert, my can emptied. My new best mate reached into the Esky and cracked another one open for me. That was the only time I took my eyes off my drink for the entire trip. My can always sat between my legs when

I was driving, and that was the only one I didn't get out of the Esky myself.

I had a few swigs and it tasted just like the rest of 'em. But after ten minutes, I began to feel groggy. I didn't know what was going on. One minute I was driving down the highway normally. The next, my vision had warped. It wasn't as if this was the first time I'd ever had a few cans driving through nowhere, but it had never come to this.

As we were only a couple of hours away from Halls Creek, I told myself I could keep on plugging. If I kept squinting my eyes, I could still see the road in front of me. I put it down to a moment of fatigue caused by driving such a long distance. But I couldn't shake the feeling of incredible lethargy—it weighed me down no matter how hard I blinked.

Meanwhile, my silent passenger sat back and cracked himself another can. He didn't seem concerned at all by my reckless swerving across the road.

I don't remember anything much after that.

4

HOOK, LINE AND SINKER

When I opened my eyes I was sitting in the front passenger seat of my car, my head resting at an awkward angle on my chest. What was going on?

The car wasn't moving. When I raised my head I could see it was parked on the side of a dirt highway. Judging from the position of the sun, the car was now facing in the opposite direction to the one I knew I'd been travelling.

Columns of trees lined the edge of the road—lots of trees. The landscape seemed typical of the fringe of the desert. Bunches of green grass fed by the generous wet season rains, red dirt, spindly bushes and a few stands of tall timbers.

It was just on dusk so I knew I'd lost a couple of hours in fairyland. Voices were what woke me, I realised, a man and a woman talking. I still felt groggy, and couldn't focus on what they were discussing.

I had no idea what I was doing there. My first thought was that I must have been tired and had stopped to doze off, but why was I in the passenger seat? Plus I felt so groggy and disorientated I thought there had to be some other explanation.

I got out of the car to have a look around and get my bearings. The voices were coming from behind some bushes. In my groggy state I thought that Sarah must have been there with me, that it must have been her talking to someone behind the bushes. I began calling out to her as I walked towards the voices, confused by the mystery of it all.

As I approached, the voices dropped. It flashed through my mind that Sarah and I didn't even like each other. Why would we be travelling anywhere together? But it seemed the only logical explanation. And a logical explanation was exactly what I was looking for: anything to account for why I had woken up on the passenger side of my vehicle in a complete stupor with no memory of what had occurred, when I should have been just about pulling into Halls Creek.

I'd taken my fair share of drugs in the past, both legal and illicit, but had nothing to compare with this feeling of emptiness. I felt like a ghost staring down at myself with no concept of what was real and what wasn't. No amount of concentration could fill the blanks.

I later learned that Aborigines from the area use a plant that has a stupefying effect for medicinal purposes and can only guess that this is what I'd been drugged with.

Groggily, I turned to walk back to the car, no more enlightened and even more confused. The keys were in the ignition. I got into the driver's seat, and was about to hit the gas, when I saw a figure out of the corner of my eye. In a flash, it jumped from the shadows and onto the footstools on the back of the car. I could tell it was a man by his silhouette in the rear-vision mirror, but his face was obscured by a bandana or something tied around his head.

I got out of the car, yelling at him: 'What the bloody hell's going on?' He jumped down and we began a pointless game of circling each other.

Realising the ridiculousness of the situation, I gave up and climbed back in. I really didn't care who he was or what he was doing on the back of my vehicle. I just wanted to get back to Halls Creek and put my feet up.

But as soon as I sat in the driver's seat, the man was back on the footstool. I watched as he grabbed hold of the wing on the roof rack with his hands.

If that's the game he wanted to play, I thought, I'd give him a ride to remember. So I started absolutely caning it down the dirt highway, trying to shake him off the rear. But he had a spider-like grip and didn't seem too fazed by what speeds I reached. He didn't even flinch when I slammed on the brakes and tried to throw the car sideways into the dirt.

What was he after? I had some stuff in the car; a few hundred bucks in my wallet, which was still sitting in the console, along with my bank and credit cards. There were a few cans of rum in the Esky, and my toolkits were probably worth a few grand. Plus, I had two mobile phones, and some designer clothes packed in my luggage, but nothing that would mean anything to him—no gangsta wear.

For some time we repeated the same charade—every so often I'd stop the car and chase him around, yelling at him to tell me what he wanted. He'd say nothing and I could do nothing but get back behind the wheel with an even worse dose of the shits than before. Although still disorientated I could feel the effects of the drug wearing off but could do nothing to process the absurd situation I was in.

I noticed him swinging what looked like a piece of rope with a torch attached at the end. He was waving it above his head like a midnight cowboy. That really had me scratching my head, trying to figure out who else might be watching him wave his flashy beacon in what was now almost complete darkness.

Then using a big rock he had probably picked up in one of our stand-offs around the car, he smashed the back window of my vehicle to force his way in. He then climbed over the shattered glass as if it were sand to get within arm's reach of me.

The next thing I knew we were wrestling and punching each other, bumping along the dirt highway at well over 100 kilometres per hour. He was in the back seat throwing fists wildly while I held my own up front trying to steer.

They weren't the first punches I'd taken in my life, and I was sure they wouldn't be the last. I still managed to keep one eye on the road ahead as I fended him off with a defensive forearm, but there was only so long we could keep that up for. There was no doubt we were bound to slam into a tree if we didn't roll over. In desperation, I spotted a clearing in the scrub on the side of the road and jerked hard on the steering wheel to squeeze us between the buffer of the bushes. Giving it full throttle as the tyres gripped the churned-up dirt, we were now in no man's land, off the dirt highway.

We ploughed over small trees like they were sandcastles. I didn't even slow down when a branch smashed through the windscreen and shattered it. Now the only way to navigate in between ducking or throwing punches was to stick my head out the driver's side window and quickly gauge what obstacles were flashing at me.

I knew we couldn't keep going like that. The car had to get bogged or slam into a tree eventually. When I did finally plant it in the dirt permanently, it was almost a relief. The car just dug into the sand and churned us deeper into the ground.

We both stepped from the car pretty gingerly, me out from the driver's side and him out the back on the other side. Then he just turned around and disappeared into the darkness, leaving me stranded next to my car and no closer to solving the riddle of what had just happened.

With not a clue where I was, I searched for one of the two torches I knew were packed in the back of the car. But I couldn't find either.

It was an absurd situation. I was still groggy, but I had sense enough to know that if I wanted to get out of there alive I had better stick with my car, even though it was bogged up to the axles in the desert somewhere. I collapsed in the grass and tried to process my thoughts, but I must have passed out. Nothing added up and I felt physically and emotionally drained.

* * *

What happened in the hours or days that followed was like a weird, terrible nightmare that I am still trying to piece together.

Lying in the desert in the freezing dark, drifting in and out of consciousness from total exhaustion and still feeling some effects of being drugged, I became aware of people coming and going, rifling through my car, searching for who knows what. But I recognised them: it was the same mob I'd stopped to help on the side of the road outside Kalkaringi. There was the big fella, the younger one and the guy I picked up on the highway. They were being helped by a couple of blow-ins, including a young woman who must have been the younger one's girlfriend.

I remember calling out to them: 'What do you want? Money? You can have it! My belongings? Take them! The car's bogged in the dirt—it's yours. What the fuck do you want from me?' But they didn't say a word.

Obviously they didn't know what to do with me: I was still alive, and now they were in a mess. They wanted me unconscious, so they could deal with me without having to struggle with their own consciences.

At one point I woke to find a .22 rifle shoved in my face. The little guy holding it told me I knew what they were looking for. I told the gunslinger straight that he'd better pull the trigger because I didn't know what he was going on about. I just wanted out. If he wanted to shoot me over a bloody car, he should get it over and done with or leave me alone.

But he was too gutless to squeeze the trigger and turned away. That's when I must have realised it wasn't my time to die.

Another time during the night I was woken by the girl, who asked me for a cigarette. Even in my semi-conscious state I remember thinking, *Are you off your head?* It could not have been a more surreal moment if Jesus Christ had appeared from the black sky and asked me to marry him. But I gave her a cigarette and then started really schitzing out at her for a drink of water. I was frantic for it.

The young Aboriginal fella came over with a bottle, telling me not to say anything so the others wouldn't know.

Bloody oath, buddy, your secret's safe with me!

I took an almighty swig and the next thing I knew it was daylight. Early. My car wasn't anywhere to be seen. I appeared to have been moved. I could see a hessian screen wrapped around some trees, obscuring two vehicles.

I pulled myself up and walked towards the cars. People were huddled on the grass preparing breakfast. One guy had pulled out enough food from his trayback to feed everyone twice, but I was clearly not invited. They kept up their simple strategy of ignoring me.

I told them that, if they weren't going to kill me, then they could at least tell me which direction it was to walk to the next town. They didn't have to drive me there—just point me in the right direction and I'd make my own way. Still they said nothing.

By now I had a raging thirst, so when the opportunity presented itself I collared one of the Aboriginal guys. If he didn't get me a drink, I threatened, I'd beat him black and blue. He knew for sure, by the rage in my eyes, that I meant it. He scurried off and came back soon after with a nearly full bottle of water, telling me to keep it quiet or he'd get in trouble.

What was going to happen if I did tell the others? They'd kill me? Kill him? I was starting to wish they would do both, and could only hope his precious gift of water wasn't full of knockout juice.

With no other offers to weigh up, I took a healthy gulp.

The next time I woke up, I was lying in a hole minus my lighter and cigarettes. In bare feet.

5

SEARCHING FOR THE SEARCH PARTY

It had shocked me to wake up buried, no better than a mangy dog, on what I assumed, from the harsh landscape, to be the fringe of the Western Desert. But later, when my mind had cleared, I wasn't surprised my captors had failed to kill me before depositing my limp body in the ground. They'd shown their weakness when the little guy had pointed the gun at me and didn't use it; I just hadn't expected to be left to die in a hole.

Either they thought I was dead already or they wanted nature to take care of what they didn't have the balls to do. It might turn out the same result either way, I supposed, unless I could find my own way out.

As the drugs they'd used to stupefy me wore off I began to piece together what had happened. The blackfella I'd picked up on the side of the Buntine Highway must have been involved. He'd probably slipped me something and robbed me as I was driving him across the border to Halls Creek to get petrol.

To get more familiar with my surroundings, I climbed the biggest tree I could see. From a scan of the horizon I could tell that, wherever I was, it was a completely different landscape to where I had been the day before. Or however many days it had been since being robbed. The country was a lot more barren, leaving me with the impression I was even more isolated.

I was lost, I was hungry, I was thirsty. I was still feeling the effects of whatever it was I'd been drugged with during what I assumed was the past two days. It was hot and no one, besides the arseholes who'd left me there for dead, had the slightest clue where to start looking for me. The only thing in my favour was the fact that I was Ricky Megee. I was alive and I could survive more than most.

After getting my bearings from the sun I figured due west was the best direction to find civilisation, in the hope of intersecting the highway to Halls Creek, and marched on. What I guessed was several hours into my meandering scramble, it occurred to me that I was probably walking further into the solitude of the desolate interior. To counter this I turned back east, in the hope of stumbling across a road or a river leading towards a homestead.

Although I didn't really have my senses, I thought that at least I was still breathing. After a couple of days I'd get my bearings and find a way out of there.

I couldn't see any roads, so I headed for a big rise on the horizon to get a better view. Surely if there was no sign of a town there would at least be some hint of civilisation I could aim for—a farm shed, the smoke from a fire, something to show me that someone else existed.

Wrong. Couldn't have been more wrong. Just scrub and bare earth, scattered with nothing but a few stubborn trees. I kept walking, but dehydration was setting in. There was no point complaining, as there was no water on the horizon. I had to get back up on my legs and keep searching for the search party.

The bare earth didn't offer a drop and neither did the crystal-blue sky above. As I stumbled on, I could feel the moisture being sucked out of me by the sun. My fluid levels were dropping to the point where I was not going to go anywhere without some kind of replenishment. How important is that stuff that falls out of the sky, really? I was beginning to understand the hardest way of all.

There was only one other option—somehow I was going to have to get used to the idea of drinking my own urine.

Avoid drinking piss—it doesn't taste very nice. Of course nobody drinks it for the taste, unless they're off their head, but, for those who haven't had to—try and keep it that way.

It certainly hadn't been a high priority for me when I began this strange nightmare—the thought had never entered my mind. Sure I was thirsty when I started walking, but I'd thought I wouldn't need a drink for a few hours. I was more interested in finding out what the bloody hell was going on, and getting found, than on wetting my lips with the stain of my own piss.

Now here I was trying to figure out the best method of drinking urine. It was so hot and desolate that the only alternative was licking a rock.

By mid afternoon, I was so bloody thirsty I couldn't take another step. Even if it rained, it would evaporate once it hit the ground in stifling heat. What was I meant to do without water? I'd been thirsty before, but this 40-plus heatwave made a mirage of everything and left me with nothing.

Just think and think and think, and keep walking. Concoct a plan that's better than drinking your own piss.

But I came up with no magic solution—there was none. I was only getting thirstier with each passing moment.

Don't think about it, Rick!

No, think about it. How can it be that I have to drink my own piss? That I have to piss in my own jocks and then try and swallow it?

That seemed to be my only choice. It wasn't going to rain and I'd die if I didn't get moisture of some kind tickling the back of my parched throat. And, if I thought about it, I knew the only kind of moisture available to me was the stuff inside.

This is it then, Ricko. Take your shorts off, peel off your undies and empty your bladder into them if you want to live to see tomorrow!

I decided the least unpleasant, and most effective, method of drinking my piss would be to soak my undies in urine and then squeeze them dry. After steeling myself to carry out my dirty deed, I stripped off below the waist and emptied myself. There was no other way to capture my piss besides cupping my hands, and they wouldn't hold many sips.

By the time I'd come to this conclusion, I was so bloody thirsty the thought of wringing my undies into my mouth seemed normal. Somehow I'd talked myself into it, and I didn't want to let a drop disappear.

It must have looked absurd—me standing there half-naked, pissing into my undies—but I no longer cared about appearances. My life was at stake. In any case, no one was going to see me. I wish they would have, because then I wouldn't have had to sink so low in the first place.

After taking aim at my jocks, the next step was to pick them up off the ground and clench my fists above my head, to trickle the contents into my mouth. I was robotic about the whole process and didn't stop to consider alternatives. I knew there simply weren't any. There were no two ways about it—I had to swallow my pride as well as my urine.

Hot and disgusting is how I'd describe the foul taste, like tipping chemicals into my mouth and then inhaling. It was certainly enough to make me throw up—I was dry retching as I swallowed the first mouthful.

There was absolutely no way I could force myself to gulp another. I was defeated by my own rotten juices.

That's enough for me—I'll take my chances with Mother Nature.

But unfortunately there wasn't a cloud to be seen and I knew that, if I didn't find water soon, I'd have to somehow drink from my sweaty, piss-stained jocks again. I was keeping an eye on the sky and looking in rocks and holes, in the hope of licking a trickle of water; but I found nothing. Nothing that resembled a search plane above me and no moisture to be found in the ground beneath my feet to save my life.

Already my feet were pretty bloody sore and bleeding. I cursed again the little pricks who had dumped me out there, for not giving me at least a decent crack at walking out with my boots strapped on. Geez, I wish I had my boots. They'd even taken my leg brace. How low was that?

Little cuts on the soles of my feet opened up in the rugged terrain, as I followed the rough tracks that appeared randomly and led to who knows where. What was I doing out there? And where were my boots? I felt like my feet had almost detached themselves from the rest of my body. They bled more profusely as the hours passed.

I wasn't in total despair—I still thought I would be rescued soon—but the challenges were getting pretty fierce. How much further does a man have to walk before he escapes or capitulates?

At that stage I wasn't really thinking about who had put me in this situation or why. My sole focus was on survival.

Surely they'd found my car abandoned. My ex-girlfriend was expecting to see me back in Port Hedland—maybe she'd reported me missing. The people at Centrelink must have been wondering what happened when I didn't turn up for my new job—people must be asking each other what happened to Ricky Megee.

The sun sank low in the sky. It had been bloody hot through the day; now it was getting cold, and there was not much time in the comfort zone between these two extremes. All I wanted to do was keep walking, find a road and get out of there. I'd walked miles throughout the afternoon, but the thought of sleeping hadn't crossed my mind.

As dark fell, a quarter moon shed some light on the path ahead, but not enough to prevent my feet from banging into rocks and branches that littered the ground. I finally accepted I'd have to build a camp for the night. Unless I stopped to rest, I was bound to trip over something and do myself a serious injury.

Standing on a rise overlooking the sparse desert, I spotted a gully with a big clump of trees not too far away. That was all I needed to camp for the night, and I hobbled over to reassure myself.

The collection of spindly trees appeared healthy enough. I pulled handfuls of smaller branches off the trunks to form a roof, which spanned a couple of metres, supported by one more solid branch that ran down the middle. It measured longer than me, but wasn't as sturdy. I stacked one end with more leafy branches, to better protect the top half of my body from the elements, and then, after spending the best part of an hour at this task, finally crawled underneath, tired out from the day's effort.

Huddled up in a little ball among the foliage, I felt so buggered that I could hardly sleep. The bottoms of my feet ached pretty bad, and my head still felt a bit funny from being drugged.

It was probably approaching midnight when the first drops of rain penetrated my improvised shelter. The previously bright stars were hidden by rolling thunderclouds, which rained steadily for what felt like a good hour. A stream of water slid along the central branch of my shelter, pouring over the edge right near my gaping mouth.

A replenishing drink of water was an incredible relief. I cupped my hands and gulped down as much as I could. The rest just disappeared into the earth before my eyes. Any raindrops I couldn't cup in my hands or catch in my mouth as they fell from the sky completely evaporated.

Still, I felt confident of finding my way out. After coming so close to death in a matter of a few debilitating hours, I knew I had to think fast and couldn't underestimate the elements. I couldn't waste my time dwelling on what had happened.

The swirling wind ripped through my branches rather more destructively than I'd anticipated. I didn't know much about the desert seasons before setting out from Brisbane. But I figured it being the wet season I could expect the odd downpour, if not daily then at least every few days. What I didn't count on was how cold the temperature dropped to at night. It was near freezing. Half the branches were torn off my buckled shelter during the night, leaving me scrambling to find cover. The canopy of the trees in the gully also was pretty poor protection from the chill of the wind, but it was better than no protection at all.

Picking up my branches as they blew off in the wind was never part of my grand plan. Clearly this shelter business was hard work if you didn't think it through thoroughly. Welcome to the reality of shaping a shelter in the desert. Getting wet and filthy to stay warm and dry sucked.

I managed to squeeze in a couple of uninterrupted hours of sleep, before waking up with the rising sun. My ankles seized up almost as soon as my eyes opened—I knew I'd have to walk that off or I was fucked; I'd simply die sitting there.

My ramshackle camp had served me pretty well during the night, except the half that blew away in the wind. That was simple enough to fix—next time I'd just use more branches.

All I could find to drink from were a few rocky crevices filled with small puddles to lap up. I went down on all fours like a dog to reach them. Burying my face in the shitty soiled stones, I dug up traces of water—enough to keep me going for a few hours anyway. There wasn't another drop to be seen that looked more satisfying.

Although it was still early morning, the temperature felt as if the mercury had already pushed through the 40-degree barrier. There was no chance of any relief from the weather.

I was determined on that second day in the desert to walk east until I found help. And maybe I would have got further if the soles of my feet hadn't been so cut up. The constant scraping from the rocks was beginning to wear away my resolve to persist with the plodding.

Reality clicked in soon enough, but not my full mental capabilities. Lumbering on further east, I kept having to sit down and take a break as the gaping cuts on my feet were sliced open. A multitude of rocks kept slipping in between my swollen toes, grinding away at my skin and my patience.

I began hating the world for my predicament, but I wasn't exactly sure why. I didn't know how my life had dissolved into this puddle of nothing.

My thoughts turned momentarily to the bastards who dumped me there. Briefly overwhelmed with anger, I figured if I could find my way back without anyone noticing I could track them down myself and discover their motives.

To take my mind off the loneliness I just walked, and walked. I only stopped to sort out my rock-infested feet, or to survey the landscape for a sign of salvation.

The contrast between my old life and what my life had become brought an occasional wry smile to my face. Here I was—the big city slicker who wore shoes all the time, always with a supporting brace strapped to my right leg since my accident—stuck out here on the fringe of the fucking desert. I had nothing but the shirt on my back and $12.30 in change tucked into my shorts.

All the debts I'd ever collected couldn't have bought me a pair of boots out here, so I couldn't see how $12.30 was going to come in handy. But I wasn't in any rush to throw the shrapnel away, just in case. I'd be able to use the cash to buy my first hamburger and strawberry milkshake when someone found me!

Just as seemingly useless were the car keys jangling in my other pocket. My car was gone, but I saw no reason to throw away the keys. They were better than having nothing. I supposed that whoever dumped me in the ground had no use for them with my car bogged up to the axles.

* * *

As that second day progressed, my thirst again became so desperate that drinking my piss seemed the only option left open to me.

My life sucks. How could it have come to this? If the wind was blowing, I'd have been pissing in it for sure, probably with my mouth open so I could swallow it up. Instead, I was debating the pros and cons of consuming my own bodily fluids. Again.

Drinking from my jocks would be more palatable this time, I reasoned. I'd tried it already and at least I knew what foulness to expect. The warmness of it, as much as the taste, put me off the first time around. I knew I couldn't stomach that again. I had to at least start thinking about different cooling methods.

After much consideration about the best approach to the worst of situations, I decided to sit my urine-soaked jocks in the shade and wait. Surely piss tasted a fraction better when it wasn't so hot?

It was a debilitating feeling, waiting for my piss-soaked jocks to cool down. Hardly something to look forward to, but at the same time it felt mildly liberating to know that my chances of survival would improve if I could just swallow a mouthful or two.

Eventually I had to stop staring and pick them up, in the hope that the taste would be better the second time around. The colour of my piss was by then a sickening deep orange, and I wondered what that signified about my health. Not that there was anything I could have done if it was a bad sign, but it was worth pondering. The lack of nutrients probably explained it, I reckoned.

With my guts clenched and my resolve solid, I once again squeezed my jocks into my mouth as quickly as possible. It hardly tasted any better, but I was more prepared and willing to suffer the consequences the second time around. I managed a few mouthfuls, before throwing my undies onto the ground in complete disgust.

At least I didn't throw up. But I had no intention of picking up my stained undies out of the dirt. I knew I couldn't drink my own piss again, even if it meant I died of thirst.

* * *

The second night my humpy was a bit stronger, half-decent even. It was basically the same design as the first, just bigger, with more branches.

After my experiences of fumbling in the dark the previous evening, I stopped walking just on dusk. I'd been following a ridge and found another patch of trees similar to the first night. But this clump was thicker, and I could pull down more foliage to make a stronger humpy.

I spent over an hour building it, using the thick foliage as insulation. The heavy branches I stacked across the top for protection from the elements. I wanted to make sure that where I slept was going to be rain-proof.

As I was building, I was thinking about how I could catch the water if it rained. I'd purposely built the enclosure so that if the heavens opened, the water would run along the main branch that sloped towards my head. I could then collect the precious drops in my cupped hands, sheltered from the bulk of the rain.

There were a few clouds scattered about when the sun went down, but nothing drastic. Because I'd been walking all day, I didn't feel like doing anything after building my humpy besides getting some rest to recuperate. I hoped for rain, but couldn't count on it. Thirst was replaced with exhaustion and I nodded off to sleep content with my branch and foliage canopy.

Some time during the night, a shower swept over the humpy and sprinkled some raindrops on my face. I woke up glad to see the water trickling down the branch near my head as I'd hoped, but I didn't get too much to drink. It didn't pour like the first night—just enough to wet my lips and wash my face really.

I wasn't sure what to make of the rain. Both nights I'd received a lashing of sorts, which I could only hope was usual for this time of year, but it hardly seemed reliable. All I could do was fill up when I had the chance and hope the next storm wasn't too many steps ahead.

The third morning I woke up early as usual and climbed to the top of the ridge, hoping to catch a glimpse of civilisation. Dark clouds were brewing on the eastern horizon; I estimated they were about 7 kilometres away, as the crow flies.

For about an hour I sat there looking out over the empty wilderness. I scanned the far corners, looking for the dust of a vehicle, but not even the wind moved. Eventually I stood up and started east, determined to reach that storm for my next drink.

Along the way I scooped out a few little puddles here and there from the night's downpour, but they were still hard work. I couldn't get my hand into most of them, they were so small. I was just able to get my nose and tongue into some and inhale what moisture I could, mixed in with a mouthful of mud.

For hours and hours I blundered on, chasing clouds that didn't appear to be moving any closer. Initially I hadn't been too concerned, figuring someone would realise I was missing and then raise the alarm. But as my situation became more desperate, so did I. A feeling of fear washed over me as I weighed up my predicament. Instead of search planes I was searching for my next trace of water. I knew though that if I entertained the thought of defeat it could swallow me rapidly. I had to stay positive and not panic.

* * *

Besides drinking my own piss, in those first few days most of my energy was directed towards trying to find somewhere comfortable to sleep when the sun went down. I kept telling myself that I could get out of there. I could climb another tree, keep going, don't stop. I was going to sort it out with whoever did this to me. Put them in a hole and see how they fared.

Keep walking in the same direction and I have to hit a road somewhere, I kept telling myself. I'd definitely hit a road.

But each time I did find higher ground, there were no roads in sight.

6

DIVINE INTERVENTION

About then is when I began to seriously think about God.

Who is God anyway? Sure, I'd always believed in God, but I'd never really thought about Him much. I imagined He'd always been around and, when I thought about it, I suppose there'd been a few occasions in my life when I'd had a touch of divine intervention without asking for it.

I'd better start believing in Him now, I reckoned. Now that I was walking through the desert without food, water, shelter or the energy to stumble to the next gut-aching view of another pointless panorama of dirt and aimless scrub.

I'd rarely gone to church growing up—just weddings and funerals basically. If now wasn't a good time to start praying for His help, there probably wouldn't be one.

It was a pretty sparse church to be initiated into—there was no one offering to bless me for my sins, no holy communion under the stained-glass windows in this neck of the woods. Just a few random trees for company and a lot of dust.

The realisation I needed help from above wasn't exactly an epiphany—more like the logical next step in the pathetic circumstances confronting me.

By the time I dropped from dehydration late on the third morning, I was pretty happy for any inspiration I could muster. I felt myself getting dizzy and weaker by the moment. I tried to keep walking, but didn't have the breath left in me. I had to stop regularly, every few hundred metres, to suck in the big ones.

My head felt like it was stuck in the clouds; my dizziness wasn't helped by the fact I hadn't eaten for four days already. My body felt ridiculously heavy with each step.

There was only so much I could take. I was literally seeing spots darting across my eyes; I was knackered.

I kept falling over, as the weight of dehydration pulled me down. I remember hitting the ground, but don't recall losing consciousness. It felt like my head became too heavy for my body, and I crashed uselessly into the earth.

The next thing I knew, I woke up in the dirt, cooking in the hot sun. I had no idea how long I'd been out for, nor what was real and what wasn't.

All I remember, after passing out, was my ex-girlfriend Julie's hand reaching out to me, her voice pleading: 'Rick! Wake up, Rick! Keep going, honey—get up, get moving.'

Julie? What was she doing here, and why was she telling me to wake up in the middle of the desert when she should be rugged up somewhere in Canada melting marshmallows?

It might not have been God talking to me, but the vision of Julie's presence was enough of a revelation to get my arse out of the dirt. I hit the track for another stint of blistering nothingness, confused but enlightened.

That experience was probably the clincher that proved to me that God helps those who help themselves. As I trudged on, still dazed, I mouthed my first prayer, asking the Man Upstairs Pulling The Strings for some sort of direction.

God, I've never prayed before, but I think I need your help. I'm not asking for a miracle—I just need a sign to show that something is out there for me. That there is a tree or a person or a God who cares that Ricky Megee lives to see another day or a decade.

Strength was something I'd left behind thousands of steps ago; it had been almost three days of trekking without result. If my prayers weren't answered soon, I'd get to see Him in person. Would I even make it to heaven, I wondered—maybe I was already in hell and this was just my initiation.

From then on water became my top priority, even more important than being rescued. My eyes were always peeled for soggy patches of earth, where I could try digging for water. Nothing escaped me.

I staggered through the sparse scrub only another couple of kilometres before finding His first sign. I'm not religious, so you can say what you want about God, but He certainly didn't muck around when I needed Him most.

I'd managed a few precious drops scraped out of the ground through the morning, but essentially I was sucking on mud. And then, a couple of hours later, with the threat of drinking my own piss again pressing hard down on me, I hit an open plain that finally offered some hope. The ground underneath felt damp and I fell to my knees to absorb as much moisture as I could, almost rolling around in the emerging swamp in pure joy.

As I followed the trail of wet patches, they turned into puddles and the puddles to sloshy channels. I could hardly believe it. Sucking up what I could as I went along, I followed the soggy path all the way to the edge of a thriving river.

It was an incredible feeling to see such a torrent of water carving its way through the desert. I couldn't believe my luck and wasted no time diving in to get my fill.

A sea of salvation in the shape of a seasonal river flowing south. I praised the Lord or whatever caused me to cross its path.

A few mouthfuls were enough, initially. I'd stumbled on a whole river, after all. There was no need to get too carried away and make myself sick.

It tasted bloody beautiful though—no mud and plenty of sustenance to liven me up. Just lying in the water felt good, too. I'd been out there for a few days without even contemplating having a bath. I'd covered some pretty rugged terrain and wanted to make the most of my good fortune.

One minute I was on the verge of death by dehydration, the next I was flapping about in the current of a river that could only take me closer to being saved. If my luck kept running like that, I'd be eating hamburgers for dinner.

I'd been thinking of having another rest to try and recuperate, but now I assumed all my troubles were solved. Fresh water, a drink, a cool respite from the heat. After that, the chance to move long distances without wearing out my poor trampled feet. The perfect solution.

But unfortunately, things don't always work out so easily.

It felt great to soothe my cuts in the flooding stream and have a drink of something besides my own piss. But when it came time to try to make my way downstream—half wading, half swimming—I found a seasonal river topped up with heavy rain was not the kind to provide an easy passage.

I didn't have to stagger over rocky ground anymore and that was great; but I did have to dodge the trees and branches buried under the water and carried by the fast-moving current.

Let me tell you that bringing your foot down on a submerged barbed-wire fence is a particularly painful way to treat your already lacerated toes. Floating can be more dangerous than fighting.

At least when you fight someone, you know what's coming. You can see their arms and legs and watch their eyes for signs of movement. Floating down the stream, there were hidden trees everywhere trapped by the floodwaters. There was no defined edge of the water, just more mud in places. I couldn't see my enemies.

I'd try to pick the smoothest route to float down, but it was impossible. Sometimes the shortest way would take twice as long because it was full of submerged trees. Sometimes I'd be swimming comfortably and crash into a shallow bank. Or I'd be walking in ankle-deep water and fall down a six-foot hole.

I just thought everything would be a bit softer on my feet, wading in the water. In reality, I was floating on top of outback cattle country, on the edge of the desert, complete with fence posts, barbed wire, debris. The river was a lot better than dehydrating in the dirt, but certainly not without its own challenges.

The river wasn't always menacing; it had its smooth channels where I could relax without fear of being clobbered. For the most part though, I had my work cut out for me.

Then suddenly around a bend a windmill appeared. Four or five hours of struggling against the river convinced me I needed to pull up and camp at this windmill. I'd had enough of floating on guard constantly.

I didn't hesitate. Anyway, I just assumed that getting rescued from there was only a matter of time. Surely someone came regularly to check the windmill—they don't build them for no reason.

I swam to the edge of the winding river and crawled out of the water, brimming with confidence. The breaks were finally going my way; someone was bound to find me.

Surrounding the windmill, a stone's throw from the river, was a lush smothering of long, green grass. Maybe I could find something to eat in there; otherwise it would provide a nice soft bed for sleeping. Beyond that was the usual bare landscape, dotted with a few random trees in the distance.

At least I knew I wasn't going to have a problem with my water supply. The torrent at my doorstep churned thousands of litres past by the second, fresh from the source.

The windmill itself looked in disrepair; the blades were missing and the rusty shell flapped uselessly in the breeze. It would make a great vantage post, though, if I climbed right to the top. I felt as if God had delivered me another precious sign.

Storm clouds seemed attracted by the sanctuary of the windmill as well. Although it wasn't raining when I arrived, they hovered above like a smokescreen from the charging sun.

After taking in my new surroundings, I climbed up the top of the abandoned shell of the windmill to yell at no one to rescue me. On the far horizon I could see a blanket of trees, but nothing to indicate habitation. Maybe a blast of dust from a distant station hand's motorbike tyre would show me the way home.

Peering from above also provided me with the opportunity to have a good scout around for the missing windmill blades. They had to be around somewhere—a windmill with no blades was a stupid idea. But they were hidden in the shadows somewhere, beyond my reach.

Climbing to the platform on top of the windmill was also a good way to escape the blanket of mozzies that were camped out down below. Thick as thieves, the little black bastards were everywhere.

The swarm thinned out if I clung to the top of the windmill, but there were still plenty of them determined enough to sniff me out and suck on my blood at a great height. How a mosquito knew I was hiding all the way up a windmill I don't know, but it pissed me off. They gave me no relief.

* * *

Mozzies. How do you describe those little blood-sucking bastards without swearing too much and bringing up buried emotions of utter hatred?

I know, I know—they're only doing their job. But there were so many of them out there doing it, out in the middle of bloody nowhere, managing to keep out of the blistering sun throughout the day somehow. Then they'd swoop in the calm of the night. I couldn't help but despise them.

Where the bloody hell they hid in the sunlight hours I couldn't tell, but I sure wanted to find out. Maybe I could learn to be just as reclusive in the dark as they were in the heat of the day.

Fat fuckin' chance! They'd been into me from the word go.

They weren't as bad in the rocky part of the bare desert. The first couple of nights wandering across the desert plains, they didn't worry me too much. I was still trying to regain my senses and process the hopeless situation I found myself in, so the mozzies were more of an annoyance than anything.

But as the drugs wore off and I found the river and the windmill, I began to realise what I might be up against. Mountains of mozzies attached themselves to my skin. I could feel them biting through my clothes and had nothing to defend myself with except my tired arms, swinging relentlessly to fight them off.

Closer to the river, the mozzie level picked up another level or ten—the water seemed to attract mozzies like a magnet. It became feeding time at the zoo as soon as the sun went down, but unfortunately I was the only one invited over for dinner.

I've camped out in the bush and at the beach a lot, but I've never seen mozzies in such intimidating numbers as in the desert. I could literally feel them sucking the blood out of me. I can't wait to go camping next time and hear someone say, 'Geez, the mozzies are bad out here.' If only people knew how bad they really can be.

At their peak my biggest concern wasn't so much the volume of mozzies, as the various new species that wanted to join in on the action. First there was one type, then two types, then four types, then five different types of the little bastards trying to suck the blood from my veins.

The first ones I encountered, as I staggered across the stone country, were your typical suburban mozzie in size and shape. The only noticeable difference to the ones back home was these were light brown in colour.

They would have rated about 3 Stars out of 5 on the Bloody Hell barometer. They weren't too drastic to deal with—more of a pain in the arse than relentless robbers of my dwindling energy. I could still see my skin, so there weren't swarms of them. Their bites didn't sting any more than what I've experienced at a backyard barbecue.

But then this breed was joined at the river by their swampy cousins, the standard black buggers. Another brown type also turned up; it seemed to be bigger and bitier than the first two types combined. I started to wonder how I was meant to stop them from latching onto me.

The black ones would have registered a paltry 2 Stars on the Bloody Hell barometer. They didn't bother me too much at all, but I certainly knew they were there.

I wasn't so lucky with the bigger brown ones though—they rated a good 4 Stars for sure. It was easy to tell when one of those big suckers landed by the impact of them piercing my skin. They would guzzle what felt like a decent lemon-squeeze worth of my blood into their guts with each penetrating raid.

I could hear them approaching from a fair distance away. I always knew what was coming, but the lack of suspense made it no less debilitating when they did sink their fangs in.

Even when I jumped into the river, there were two or three different varieties that wanted a piece of me. The rest of my body could be underwater, but to them that still meant my face was fair game. I had to splash and duck to dodge the dive-bombing, trying not to get my feet caught in a tree or a fence in the current.

There was no avoiding them, no matter where I tried to hide.

* * *

I decided to sleep huddled on top of the windmill's elevated platform, the first night there. It was late afternoon by the time I arrived via the river and the mozzies had settled in before I could find the blades for shelter. There were no trees within range to build a decent humpy from, either.

The clouds were threatening, but it wouldn't matter where I slept. There was no shade to hide under anywhere besides the thin sliver of the windmill.

To sleep, I stretched out on the windmill platform, careful not to roll over the edge and into thin air and the hard thud of the ground 20 metres below. I figured that when that sun came up in the morning, and the mozzies disappeared down below, I'd build a proper fortress.

The next morning the rain was torrential. I managed to sleep through most of the night without falling off my perch, but the clouds had to burst eventually. When they did, just after sunrise, they did so in symphony. Still, with no better offers, I stayed glued to my elevated seat.

After a good hour of searching, I spotted the windmill blades from high above, shining through the sheets of pelting water. That was the break I needed—I could now build a proper shelter. I clambered down the shell of the slippery windmill, keen to get to work on my new humpy.

The blades looked like they'd been abandoned, just like me. There were more than a dozen of them all stacked up in the long grass on the other side of the paddock, about a hundred metres from the base of the windmill.

Each of them a couple of metres long, they looked irresistible. While I wasn't quite sure what to do with them, I felt glad to have some waterproof building materials to work with.

This became my first properly built humpy. I didn't start with any particular shape in mind—I just wanted to make it as rain- and mozzie-proof as possible. Only then could I worry about the comfort factor.

I spent the whole day working on my tepee-like temple. The rain hardly stopped and neither did I, packing in mud between the crevices and plugging holes inside with grass.

My design consisted of the windmill blades formed like a pyramid. I laid a couple of protective blades across the top as extra support beams, and they kept out most of the moisture. The dirt floor still got damp around the few spots where the rain dripped down through the cracks, but it held up reasonably well in a downpour.

Four days I spent packing in the holes from the inside and out, trying to shore up the foundations. The work was mind-numbing, but at least it gave me something to do during daylight hours.

By the time I finally finished piecing the blades together, it looked like something you could propel to outer space. All these fans were poking out at strange angles; there was mud packed up at the entrance and clumps of grass stuffed in between the gaping holes. It was certainly a weird construction, but it worked wonders in the circumstances.

* * *

It just rained and rained and rained at the windmill; there was never even a glimpse of good rescue weather. I spent so much time in the pelting rain on top of that windmill, looking for lights or some sign of movement, I began to feel like a windmill. The frustration of not getting anywhere weighed me down.

I still climbed to the top of the platform regularly, to keep my hopes up, but the stark panorama always remained the same. Only the occasional small plane in the far distance provided the faintest hope of rescue. Oh, to be on that plane, or at least noticed.

A seasonal river and a few drops of rain were a great outcome when I'd been dying of thirst. But four days of torrential storms had stretched the friendship a little too far, I thought. After all, I'd only wanted a drink of something besides my own piss. Instead, I'd been served up a drought-breaking flood that threatened to wipe me out.

The torrential supply of fresh water meant the only food I could scrape for nourishment was a few different types of grass, covered in a thick layer of mud. After a couple of days of killing time at the windmill, my hunger had got the better of me and I had begun scraping around to swallow anything that looked remotely edible. Everything was wet grassy crap—nothing flash—but I had to give it a try because I began to get obsessed about food and not eating. If I didn't eat grass, what else was there to stomach?

It didn't matter how much I shoved in my mouth or how starved I was, the grass still tasted like rain-saturated grass. The depressing texture of soggy mud couldn't be dressed up. Eventually, I'd consumed so much of the rain-saturated crap, but it did nothing to satisfy my growing hunger pains.

I was also suffering from the horrendous cold at night. And the faraway drone of a plane never came closer, despite my constantly reminding God in my solemn prayers each night that my eyes and ears were peeled for someone to show an interest in my survival.

After four days of standing around in the puddles waiting for a sign, I finally decided a proactive approach might be required. If He'd given me water and a windmill when I really needed it, who knew what could be next?

At least I'd learned how to stay sort of dry and keep the mozzies out with some success. But, as it turned out, there wasn't much respite for my suffering feet at the windmill. It was soggy and wet all the time, and my feet were still cut up and bleeding.

I had some pain in my ankles, but that paled into insignificance when compared to the weeping infection attacking my feet. The water did a good job flushing out the wounds, but they couldn't heal properly with all the moisture.

On the bright side, the rest at the windmill did do some good for my weary legs. They weren't as tired and sore as they had been when I arrived on the cusp of total collapse.

The kilometres they felt capable of carrying me offered some hope.

I was also starting to get pretty bloody hungry after not eating for more than a week. Originally food wasn't really an issue as finding water and being rescued were my only priorities. But, as the days dragged on, my hunger became a gnawing obsession.

Nevertheless I remained 100 per cent confident of getting out alive. The possibility of death had not seriously crossed my mind.

* * *

With nothing but rain and soggy grass sandwiches minus the bread, plus the occasional plane miles away as the only sign of encouragement, it was clear no one was coming to get me from the windmill. I would have to find my own way out.

As a farewell effort I shaped an SOS sign out of the windmill blades that could be clearly identified from above. My humpy pulled apart quite easily and, when the blades were placed in formation next to the windmill, they looked quite effective.

After pointing the sign in the general direction I was headed, I jumped back into the river. Surely it would eventually cross a road or go under a bridge. It couldn't just stop. But what if it just spat me out in the middle of the desert?

I had to take the risk. With no sign of being rescued, it was time to leave my space-shuttle fortress and float away.

7

THE BIG RED GATES

It was quite tranquil floating down the river. The sparsely vegetated environment provided a harsh contrast to the gentle flow of the water and my mind again drifted to thoughts of being saved. How it would happen, I wasn't sure. But it would happen.

Just as I was thinking that perhaps there was no end to the ever-winding river, bang—I hit a track.

I'd been in the river for about four hours when the track floated into view. It had been getting colder and colder in the water—too cold for comfort. Worst of all, I didn't want to take the risk of being deposited on a massive salt plain a hundred miles from anywhere.

Now all I had to do was jump out of the river and the track would lead me to civilisation. It had to be there for a reason—people didn't just carve a track down to the river for the hell of it, did they?

I'd already discovered back at the windmill I had to be careful what I wished for, even stuck out in the desert.

I was hoping the river would lead to a house or a truck stop. Instead, in His own inscrutable way, God delivered the track to me.

Not exactly what I was aiming for, of course, but enough to keep me staring up towards the sky for some hint of a rescue plane or helicopter. It also kept pace with my theory that God was not going to serve me a steak on a silver platter—I'd have to prove myself to Him before polishing the plastic cutlery at the roadhouse.

Whether He was listening to me or not, I felt glad that something kept on happening. The track must be the next piece of His puzzle.

I paddled over to the calm water's edge with a welcome feeling of relief washing over me. That optimism soon wore off, though.

Pounding the hard earth again, instead of swanning down the river, all too soon I was reminded how important water was when I was stuck in the middle of nowhere. There one minute and gone the next. Here I was—hour after hour of one foot after the other on the track, with not a hint of rain or water to soothe my aching feet or cracked lips—when, only the day before, I'd been cursing the seeping clouds.

There were just a few puddles on the side of the track to sustain me once I left the river and its marshy fringes. The countryside became drier and drier, until there was nothing but bare earth again.

Geez, I wish I had my river. Why did I leave all that water behind me?

A couple of hours into the walk, just when I began to contemplate going back in search of the river again, I discovered the main track. The countryside still resembled the sparsely vegetated dust bowl I'd been walking through since leaving the river, but it looked more promising. A few clumps of thirsty vegetation hidden among the spindly grass showed a hint of humanity.

I only had to wander down the track for a few more kilometres before I stumbled on a fence. And not just any fence—this was a real property fence, with impressive red gates and a big sign on it.

The sensation of setting eyes on a property sign that someone else had put there was one of pure amazement. All that walking had paid off; my heartache soothed instantly. The sign on the fence was as long as a truck, announcing that I'd arrived in Heytesbury Beef Country—wherever the hell that was.

The sudden euphoria obscured the burden of reality, temporarily. *Pray to God, I'm saved.*

I'd been stuck out there for a week already; finally it felt like I was getting closer to being found. For a moment I forgot about all the shitty things I'd had to endure and allowed myself a few deep sighs of relief.

How I'd dreamed of being rescued! I didn't care how it happened, but big red gates were my best sign yet that I was near a homestead. I absorbed my good fortune and set my sights on the road ahead, hoping it was a short one.

I couldn't let myself get too excited by the signs of civilisation, or else I'd be more disappointed if things didn't work out. All I concentrated on was making sure I made the right decisions to improve my chances of survival.

Then you start to wonder how big a cattle station really is. Is it two hundred square kilometres, or three thousand? I didn't know. I hoped I wasn't in the middle of it, if that was the case.

I was getting incredibly hungry. I knew I wasn't starving to death; not yet, anyway. But my guts were certainly aching.

There were a few calves and cows wandering the scrub— plenty of beef meandering about—but, at that stage, cow slaughtering remained a last resort. They looked like too much effort, and I still felt confident I'd be saved pretty soon.

Taking the hefty bovines out of the equation, there wasn't much wildlife to consider along the way, except for a few different flowers to eat. Some were decent enough and others tasted like shit, but nothing worth spewing up. They filled a small hole and kept me occupied.

Maybe my hunger would be sorted beyond the big red gates. The dirt road beyond them made the path I'd been following look like a mere goat track in comparison. There were now plenty of puddles on the verge of the road as well. I couldn't believe my luck and was eager for a sample. The water was muddy, but it tasted a lot better than drinking piss from my jocks. The sun was shining on my sorry arse for a change.

Up until now had all been a test, today was the day. I wasn't stopping until I found a house or a highway.

* * *

I'd walked a good 6 kilometres or so from the river to reach the big red gates and now I was paying for it. Blood was

74

pouring from my feet again and both of them were hurting. The right one was chopped up more, so I began favouring that side. Which only shifted the problem to my left ankle.

There was a constant burning pain in my feet that I could no longer ignore. They were all cut open and bleeding continuously. I tried not to exacerbate the situation by looking at them. A few hundred metres down the road past the big red gates, the idea hit me to wrap my feet in my t-shirt as extra padding from the scorched earth.

The ground was hard underfoot; it felt like hot cement. So I hugged the edge walking along the dirt road where it felt mildly cooler. But while the mud was slippery and soft on the surface, it only managed to conceal the rough gravel underneath that ravaged my poor feet just as much.

Ripping my t-shirt in half, I bound both my feet carefully, before resuming the long slog down the road. The t-shirt seemed to work pretty well as a cushion; the pain still nagged at me, but I could walk further without grimacing. It was the only shirt I had and tearing it in half to use as padding for my feet meant bearing the full brunt of the sun on my body. But if I didn't do that, I couldn't walk, so the decision was easy. I'd just have to put up with the constant sunburn.

My bright idea proved even more effective where there was any stagnant water lying about in the washouts that lined the side of the road. I could then soak the rags before wrapping my feet up again.

There were a few things that pissed me off with my rag wraps, though. Nothing is ever that simple. If my feet were wet, the moisture would collect little pebbles in between the rags as though they were magnets. That made it especially unbearable if the sun then dried the rags out and the material shrank tight around my skin. It felt like little ball bearings were rolling around in my socks—and that would force me to stop and undo the rags, to brush the small stones off. I was forced to do this more times than I care to remember.

Tie them up again. Walk a few kilometres. Stop. Brush, tie, walk, limp, stop. Brush, clean, shake, tie, walk. This was my routine to keep moving. Sometimes the rags would just come loose and I'd have a different reason to stop hiking.

It was not only a pain in the arse, but painful, having all those ball bearings rubbing against my feet. On a bad stretch, my feet would be left red raw from the rocks ripping away at the skin—not an impediment I needed when I was trying to walk to civilisation, wherever that was.

Eventually I couldn't go any further than a kilometre without having to pull up to nurse my feet, or rewrap the sodden rags. I felt as if I couldn't make it much further physically; but then, if I didn't keep walking, there was no way I was going to get out alive.

My best way to overcome this tyranny of distance was to occupy my mind with something else besides reality so I could get on with the job of walking. Bad songs, movie lines, survival techniques I'd seen on television—anything to focus on other than the pain of my feet.

Slowly my mind lulled my body into a false sense of security, turning my legs of jelly into solid rocks of attrition. It's funny how your pain threshold stretches like that when you're faced with such extreme situations. At first my feet were really painful—all chopped up and bleeding and requiring constant attention. As they became worse from the wear, the pain wore off, until the result was more niggling than excruciating. I kept telling myself to just keep going and block it out—the pain's bearable. *Keep walking while you can and worry about the effects of it all later.*

If only I had my CAT boots, the pair sitting in the back of my car somewhere. Put those on my feet and I would've gladly walked all the way back to Queensland.

Rolling my ankles while power-walking hurt, but not enough to stop me in my tracks. All pain was relative.

Keep walking and find water, Rick, or you are going to die.

All I had to support me was the walking stick I had picked up on the track leading from the river to the big red gates. Because my feet were killing me, almost as soon as I jumped out of the river I started keeping an eye out for potential walking sticks, for branches on the side of the track that might be able to take my weight.

I had tried other sticks before finding the one that carried me through much of my travels. The first one broke on me almost straight away. It cracked down the middle when I applied the slightest pressure, before splitting completely. Others were just the wrong size or felt uncomfortable to handle.

It sounds a lot easier than it really was to find the right one. My rotten ankle was causing intense pain and my feet were all cut up and bloodied. I wanted to make sure I chose the right piece of wood as my support and walking companion. Without a decent stick, I was fucked. I simply wouldn't be able to keep up the pace required to find my way home.

Suddenly, my perfect stick appeared among the rubble of broken scrub. It was the right length for my height and the right thickness to fit in the palm of my hand—all I had to do was to snap the little bits off the end to make a fork I could grip for more stability. It just felt perfect and did everything I could ever ask of a walking stick.

It sounds a bit weird to say I made friends with a simple piece of wood. But I was pretty short on company out there and my stick never let me down.

At first its purpose was all about relieving my aching feet, but in the end that piece of dead wood meant everything to me. As well as being a digging tool, it kept me going when I thought I couldn't soldier on any further. It was my one constant companion.

The first time my stick came in handy for something other than standing up was as I trudged down the road past the big red gates. To create a bit of shade, I decided to unwrap my feet and hook my shirt up between my stick and a tree and hide underneath for a breather. It was a welcome relief from the sweltering sunshine.

From then on, all I needed was a tree here and a branch there poking out at the right angle to create some welcome shirt shadows. My stick's versatility proved invaluable.

Slowly, the puddles petered out to virtually nothing again. I trudged further down the road beyond the big red gates.

Walking, walking, walking. It was bullshit—I hated walking.

Big red gates or no big red gates, it didn't matter how close I was to a homestead or a roadhouse. My only source of water now was filthy dugouts filled with grit and stale cowshit.

Pounding through the dirt in bare feet with temperatures touching 50 degrees, there was no escape from the baking oven. As night fell, the chill of darkness swung the thermometer to bloody freezing, and the mozzies came out to play.

For my first night past the big red gates, I just gathered up heaps of grass and cowshit on the side of the road and rolled myself up in it like a shit sandwich. It was a confusing end to a very tiring day.

What I didn't realise, until I became a big ball of shit-smelling grass, was that I'd also just wrapped myself in the mozzies hiding in there. They were very glad to see me. Grass and cowshit and mozzies in the one combination; I'd done well.

There was no point getting upset about it, though. I was beginning to understand the mozzies would find me wherever I slept and at least the grass kept me warm.

I woke up early and walked a lot the next morning, but I wasn't happy. The lack of sleep caused by fending off mozzies the previous night nagged at me and so did seeing no decent sign of rescue.

All I came across were a couple of car tyres off a scraper on the side of the road. Someone had been there with heavy machinery, but they were long gone by the time I arrived.

How far could a fucking road go for, anyway? I reckoned I could see 20 kilometres up the road and there wasn't even a bend.

The dead straight road would tease me with a rising slope that revealed the exact same panorama when I reached the rise. I seemed to be relentlessly chasing the impossible down a path to nowhere.

With nothing to do but keep moving, I felt like the human equivalent of the coyote in Road Runner. There could be a house somewhere and I wouldn't even know it. Where was the bloody homestead?

Don't leave the road, Rick. You found the road. What if you get lost? Don't get lost, Rick. That was what I kept telling myself, over and over.

What really convinced me that someone was following my progress was when I dropped from dehydration a second time. The constant crawl along the road had revealed nothing and I simply didn't have the energy to keep plugging on with nil result.

Relying on God again, I prayed for rain. Not of drought-busting proportions, but enough to collect a drink from a washout on the verge of the road or something.

Looking to the skies from down on my buckled knees, I could almost see my reflection in the crystal-blue haze. As usual when I felt so desperate, it showed absolutely no sign of answering my prayers.

But I'd learned you never know if you don't ask, so I put my order in for the gentle pitter-patter of raindrops. And, as if David had kicked Goliath squarely in the nuts, the clouds began to brew.

Within fifteen minutes it was pissing down. I couldn't believe it. I don't know what it feels like to win the lottery, but I imagine it doesn't get much better than tasting water on the back of your parched throat in those circumstances. Especially when you know it's the only thing in the whole world that will keep you alive for another day.

Even if I'd won $100 billion dollars in Lotto, I still wouldn't have been able to get a sip of water stuck out there in the desert to save my sorry arse, unless it rained. Yet here it was bucketing down, and I only had the shirt on my feet to collect the reward.

It's amazing how happy I could be about something so simple. Being able to drink mouthfuls of relatively fresh water was an absolute blessing. He just seemed to be helping me with ideas and bits and pieces to keep me going, without solving the puzzle completely.

* * *

By that afternoon, after the clouds had dried up again, I'd just about given up on the road leading me to anywhere but my own gravesite. That's when I arrived at an intersection announcing human contact, as well as a choice for me, Ricky Megee.

I'd been walking along that damn road for more than a day without a hint of anyone. I knew I wouldn't be passing through the intersection regardless of the consequences.

The intersection had two signs, pointing east and west. The signs read: BOREE to the left and WALLAMUNGA YARDS to the right. Was it a curse or a blessing?

Why would this happen to me? Why couldn't it just be a straight road?

Was the house another two hundred kilometres down the road I'd been walking along for two days? Or was it just a few hundred metres up the track to Boree? At least the signs were telling me to go somewhere—someone had planted them in the ground.

I thought I'd give both options a try, choosing to go right first, to have a look at what was on offer at Wallamunga Yards. It was all downhill in the direction of Western Australia and I wasn't overly confident; I figured that the word Yards meant it was just going to be a mustering point. But maybe it was near a station cottage. I had to check it out.

I walked and walked. There wasn't a drop of water, there was nothing to see, and it was getting hotter. This was bullshit.

When I eventually arrived at my destination, just as I feared they were worn-out cattle yards, with no tasty cows for the devouring and no sign of life. I turned back to the intersection more frustrated than ever.

I'd managed to use up more energy. It was hot; I was thirsty. I needed to set up camp and look for food and figure out which direction to go next. How come I was stuck out here and not eating hamburgers?

I had the choice between following the sign to Boree, or continuing down the road to seemingly nowhere, or taking my chances through the dirt into no man's land.

It was the middle of the afternoon and I could feel the heat boiling my blood as I went in search of a tree to provide some shade and somewhere maybe I could sneak a rest. The more energy I wasted trying to get found, the quicker I'd die. That pissed me off.

Even more annoying was always having no food and water in the heat of the afternoon. Always the time when I needed it most and was least likely to go looking. There were no quick fixes out here, Ricko—only fucking curses.

I couldn't rest, though, because I was thinking about the planes I had seen and heard in the far distance at the windmill. To improve my chances of rescue, I made another SOS sign out of rocks at the intersection, pointing in the direction I intended to walk—heading east down the road to Boree.

If this was my last brilliant idea, then I was going to make it count. I collected armful-sized boulders, as if they were pebbles, and created my rocky lifeline to the pilots patrolling the skies above. It took a couple of hours slugging through the scrub in search of enough ammo to finish my second SOS to the world. Blind Freddy could see I needed help.

Hunger was gnawing away at me. I channelled the adrenaline inspired by my rock-scavenging effort to fuel a food run, sensing that things were finally happening in my favour.

Go find food while you still can, Rick! Witchetty grubs are hiding in the trees. Keep doing things to help yourself and you'll be rewarded. Birds would have tasted all right too, but they were far too clever for me; they flapped their wings and flew off to freedom the second I showed a passing interest.

If only I had had a sniff of the unbearable pain about to smack me in the face. I would've happily walked down the road to Boree on a grumbling stomach.

8

GUT INSTINCT

With no hint of what was to come, I followed my gut instinct and went searching for a juicy grub. I reckoned I'd find them for sure in one of the hollow logs poking out of the sun-drenched landscape. The bright red dirt didn't offer much hope and the light smattering of scrubby trees looked as thirsty as me.

I wasn't really sure where to start looking, but spotted a dead tree that fitted the part. It was just off the track and looked like it had been hit by lightning, its charred exterior protecting a hollow inside.

A hollow log—the perfect hidey-hole for a whole family of fat chewy grubs. Without hesitating, I stuck my left hand inside the rotten stump to feel around for a fistful of the delightful little suckers. I could almost taste them in my mouth and feel them slithering down my throat.

Fishing in that hollow and up to my armpit in sifted dirt, I felt a pinch. Something latched onto my left ring finger. The little prick bit me!

As the seconds passed, the pain increased. I soon realised why when I pulled my hand out. I was holding a fucking bush centipede, two fingers fat and 20 centimetres long, with a big evil red head on him.

I didn't know whether to eat him, or bite him back. But I reckoned he'd caused me enough grief and was probably full of poison.

The first tree I stick my hand into and I get bitten. I haven't killed anyone lately—so what's the go here?

I tossed the evil thing aside in disgust as the finger he had chewed on started swelling up. Soon enough, my hand ballooned and my whole arm bloated.

I panicked as the pain raced up my arm. I couldn't sit there; I needed to find a doctor.

I looked again at the sign pointing to Boree and made a run for it. Surely it couldn't be that far to this place Boree—I'd die on this road otherwise. *The dingoes will eat me; I've gotta find a doctor.*

I'm not sure if it was the pain of the centipede bite that caused me to perform some kind of delirious rain dance, but I just took off down the track. I was screaming, yelling out that I needed help, I needed an ambulance. *There's gotta be a house out here somewhere. Someone must be able to hear my cries of desperation.*

It was the first time I truly believed I was going to die from something other than exposure. For sure, the consequences had to be permanent with such a degree of feverish pain racking my body.

The intense poison shooting through my entire body was excruciating. I seriously thought I was done for—done in by a fat fucking bush centipede in the middle of nowhere. The left side of my body throbbed as I careered down the track, screaming for mercy. Where the road to Boree led I no longer cared.

The pain became blinding as the sun set. I didn't know what to do. In my frenzy, I thought I saw a light off in the distance and abandoned the track I was on, and took off across the bare paddock.

I was blinkered only by my intense misery. Somehow I was convinced I could take a short cut to medical attention. I needed a fucking doctor like I needed a miracle.

It wasn't just the physical hardship wearing me down. Just as confusing was my mental descent. As I chased what I thought were those headlights constantly flickering out of reach, I could no longer tell whether they were my last ray of hope or the first sign of my madness.

Those lights seemed to dance and dart through the night sky and I charged for them. I was so focused on their sporadic movements that I fell face down into two separate fences concealed in the darkness.

The first time this happened, the harsh impact of barbed wire sat me on my arse pretty quick. I was stunned for a moment, but I regained my feet even more determined to find my way. Then I did the same thing again to another one further along the paddock.

I thought these two fences might have been there to keep the cattle out of the yard of the homestead. To catch someone's ear, I started yelling out in the darkness even more frantically.

In the delirium of chasing down what I thought were car lights, I'd completely lost contact with the only track I knew. *Where's the road? I need to find the road.*

I couldn't see much as I blundered through the bush at night at the best of times. Now stumbling into big mudholes and kicking logs with monotonous regularity, I was injuring myself at every step. Yelling at the distant car lights, my eyes started going funny. Maybe I should've stayed on the track.

Walk faster. Something's not right—I don't feel very well, I need to sit down.

Lying in the cool grass was the only relief available. This time the tears running down my face had nothing to do with being dumped and forgotten, and had everything to do with the daggers of venom the centipede had released into my hunger-ravaged body.

As the hours passed during the night, the left side of my neck and my face swelled up as well. I could feel the build-up of fluid gently choking me. Of course there were no cars, no doctor and no solution to my depressing situation. It was just another set of ridiculous circumstances to endure alone. For a time I continued to press on through the darkness.

Maybe it was four hours after I was poisoned—maybe it was ten—but eventually I gave up on finding the car and plumped down in the dirt for the final time, waiting to die. Collapsed under a tree, I felt I was done for. I knew it—nothing or no one could save me from an excruciating end.

It was the raindrops that woke me. I felt them splattering my spread-eagled body, shaking me from what I thought was a permanent slumber. When I wiped my eyes instinctively, I realised my arm didn't sting. I could feel my whole face and even manage to scrunch my little finger without grimacing.

I'm alive and wet. My lucky day! Just when I expected to die, I'd received a sign to continue my journey deeper into despair and was replenished with a drink for good measure.

Where did that car go? Which way was I walking? I hope that lightning on the horizon is not what I thought the car lights were.

Get your shit together, Rick. I had felt pretty sure it was a car but, when I reached the top of a nearby hill, I looked out over a plateau of sparse trees and bushes, with no suggestion of lights to be seen.

I'd been chasing lightning bolts for sure. What a dickhead! To add to my woes, I'd gone completely off course and was more lost than ever.

Now there was no sign of the Boree intersection, or a decent track even. I was stuck in the middle of a paddock the size of a suburb when my aim was to get back to the Boree track and discover wherever it was the sign pointed to.

At least I felt better. I just had to stay away from the hollow logs and come across some water.

There was nothing to guide me but some old car tracks trampled by cattle hooves. These sprouted a few dodgy waterholes not even I would drink from.

Cow tracks. Cows generally know where they're going—I wondered if they were heading to get a feed from the station house. Wishful thinking!

I planted my feet into their well-trodden imprints with an air of confidence that evaporated by the empty kilometre. Where the bloody hell were these cows going? They left me their tracks, but nothing else.

Not very encouraging, but at least it was something positive as the light of a new day began to dawn. I couldn't complain—this's what you get for leaving the road in the first place.

Then my hunger began gnawing at me again. With no substantial food in my stomach for the previous ten days, it had become pretty savage as the pain of the centipede bite subsided. Eating grass and roots wasn't enough to even come close to satisfying me. I could stomach eating the grass better than drinking my own piss, but I didn't want to live on it. What else could I eat?

The few scattered trees provided little insight to my location and were absorbed by the monotonous backdrop of spindly grass. There was nothing to indicate that anyone would visit that part of the station—not even a stray cow. My hunger was insatiable and, with not a grain of food in sight, I prayed to the Man Upstairs to help me out. Again He came through in the form of a random patch of bush flowers, little purple ones with red trimmings. I found them blooming brightly in the dirt after crawling behind some bushes to hide from the blistering heat that signalled the start of a new day.

I digested them immediately, without even thinking of the consequences. They didn't taste too bad either. Not a smorgasbord, but enough to keep me going for a while longer. Were they poisonous? Would I throw up and die if I ate one? I didn't care.

Pulling the flowers intricately apart, I spotted the little bugs that lived on them. Maybe the little bugs were tasty too.

Are you going to start eating little bugs, Rick? Has your life come to this? No, not quite yet, but eating bugs wasn't far away.

The stupid things you think about when you're starving and thirsty, either freezing cold or boiling hot, lost in the desert. Already I'd dropped several times, but at least I was still alive. I was getting somewhere. I felt half dead, but a blackfella would have found a way out of there, so there had to be one.

I was surviving; it wasn't my time to die.

Eventually, I stumbled on one of the fences I assumed had felled me in my delirious state the previous evening. I figured my best chance of finding my way out would be to follow a new set of cow tracks that had appeared and ran parallel to the fence posts. I assumed they would take me to the track that would lead me back to the Boree intersection.

That sign had said Boree, so there had to be something down there. Why else would there be a sign pointing to it. But was the sign actually saying Boree or Bore E? Did I read it right, or was I walking towards a bore?

Always questioning myself without answers. I was tired, I was hungry, I was thirsty and I had come to the realisation I was probably going to die out there. *Shit, it's hot!*

For added inspiration, I began calling myself Boree Megee. I just wanted to find my way back and get on with the job, so I tried to encourage myself any way I could. To keep my spirits up, I set myself endurance challenges. I'd pick a point in the distance and use all my energy reserves to reach it in the hope of finding the station house on the next horizon. All my thoughts centred on locating another living person. Each time I was disappointed I'd block it out by setting another point and trying again.

It surprised me how far I must have staggered when I was filled with the centipede's poison. I thought it was pretty good going for someone in my condition.

Towards evening I found a patch that was all wet and sloppy from the mud and cowshit, but where were all the cows that would lead me to food and water? The stench was overbearing, but it might make a good mudhouse.

Once again I covered myself in mud to create warmth for the night—a constant smothering. I hoped I wouldn't get sick from having that shit on my face. Mud and cowshit covered my entire body—my face and hair was completely caked in the crap.

I smelt and tasted like cowshit, and I was building a cowshit house topped with handfuls of grass and sticks. But it didn't work—it didn't keep the mozzies away. I was not a happy lad, and whoever put me there was going to know all about it when I made my way out.

It smelt putrid and I was still getting attacked by mozzies. But the stinking warmth it provided that night from the unrelenting desert chill gave me some kind of relief. Who would have thought it gets so fucking cold in the desert that a shit blanket becomes a worthy option?

My cowshit mud barricade stood about 60 centimetres tall by the time I'd finished constructing it and crawled inside for a much-needed sleep. The absurdity of smelling like a dirty cow's arse certainly wasn't lost on me, but I couldn't see the funny side anymore. Life had become a bad joke, frankly. I was getting eaten by mozzies and drinking muddy shitty water to stay alive; lying in shit, rubbing it over my body. What the hell was I doing out here?

A cow mud shit house full of mozzies that didn't stop biting me—what's next? When I tried to kick the mozzies off me as I lay huddled inside my humpy, my foot exploded through the roof. Why bother even repairing it?

Mozzies was the simple answer to that question. Rain had started falling and I was slipping and sliding all over the place, trying to gather some more grass and branches to patch up my roof in the rain. But it was useless.

When it all became like too much hard work, I curled up into a ball on the ground of my humpy and closed my eyes to shut out my shelter troubles. Fuck this—they couldn't annoy me when I was asleep.

I couldn't believe I was huddled in the bush like a long-grasser sleeping rough. All my mates would be out drinking and eating hamburgers, living it up large. Normally I'd be the life of the party, cracking jokes or telling stories. But I tried not to dwell on what I could be doing and instead concentrated on what I had to do to increase my chances of getting out alive.

Finally I drifted off to sleep. Only to wake up in the middle of the night with an incredible thirst. It was no longer raining but there was no surface water around, only the settling dew on the ground. In desperation I dragged my shirt through the grass to collect the precious few dewdrops remaining, wringing them into my mouth and being careful not to spill any, just like I had done with my piss-soaked jocks. It felt totally liberating.

If only I could find similar relief for my feet. I'd tried combining mud and leaves in with my rags, but this didn't seem to do anything to soothe my scorched soles. I knew they would take time to heal and nothing could change that.

They were getting tougher, though. I had felt that as I soldiered on through spindly scrub or scrambling over sharp rocks. Surfaces that would once have dropped me, I could now tackle without flinching.

Stepping on little clumps of grass, with their sharp needles that pushed through the mud, no longer hurt me; but I had to pick them all out of my feet at the end of each day. If I missed even one splinter, it would pus up until I gritted my teeth and scraped into the wound with my fingernails for relief.

The satisfaction of conquering such pain was always overshadowed by my complete and utter desperation. There was no disputing the hopelessness confronting me. Only sleep interrupted my misery, but it was only ever temporary.

* * *

Daylight. Another day and another sleepless night swathed in shit. I woke up early to follow another cow track that would lead me to who knows where, staggering along thirstier than ever.

My mind was tuned to high alert for signs of rescue, but no alarm bells were ringing. Just the sad tone of my sinking spirits. I had to keep going, though. Being overwhelmed by my pathetic situation wasn't going to help me.

Today was the day, I could feel it. I kept telling myself this. *After almost two weeks of wandering the desert hopelessly*

I'll find my freedom, no matter how hard I have to fight for it.
How hard could it be to get back to the track to Boree? Just
follow the fence line across the paddock until it intercepts
the path I'd lost track of and I'd be laughing.

To really confuse the situation, I stumbled across another fence
that bisected mine. Shit, what was I supposed to do now?

I could distinctly remember being knocked on my arse
twice by fences hidden in the darkness while I stumbled
delirious from the centipede's sting. But I couldn't tell if I'd
been walking in circles—if it was the same fence I'd been
following or I'd found another one. *Think it through properly,
Rick; your life may depend on the outcome.*

As the fence line I'd been following had turned up nothing
familiar, I changed course and set out in the other direction
of the new fence. I wasn't sure if I'd made a smart choice,
but I fixed my sights on the new path ahead anyway, telling
myself I was on the right road.

My legs wore out as the afternoon wore on and I began
looking for somewhere to set up camp for the night. I didn't
want to mould another house out of shit after the dramas of
the previous evening and had my eyes peeled for a suitable
timber setting.

Coming across a big gum tree next to the fence line, I
stopped to survey its humpy potential. A large log lay across
the ground and the branches within arm's reach looked solid
enough. *I'll grab a few of those fence posts for extra reinforcement
and make a humpy out of it.*

Hoping the farmer wouldn't get too pissed about me
ripping half his fence down, I worked relentlessly for a couple
of hours. I pulled down branches and dragged them into

place, before climbing inside my new humpy to catch up on some much-needed rest.

In desperation, I again prayed to God. *Some water, God—I need to drink! I'll be the best person, I'll do anything you want, just give me a sign.*

And then it rained.

It didn't just rain; it pissed down. I watched the storm for so long I wished for it to stop raining. One minute I was that hot and thirsty, and the next it was blowing a gale and pouring rain and I was freezing cold again.

I just wanted a drink, God, not another one of Your miracles. You can stop now.

On the bright side, the rain filled up the waterholes and washed all the cowshit from the previous night clean off me. Little flowers would also spring up from the soaking once the rain settled, I reassured myself.

Unfortunately, the moisture also prompted the soldiers of nature to launch an attack of unprecedented proportions. My humpy was holding up in the elements, but what was that crawling all over my face?

Ants.

The fence posts I'd ripped out from the ground must have been full of ants, and now they were all over me. They were bursting out of the woodwork by the thousands.

I crawled out of my protective shelter, shivering and swearing. All day I'd been hot and bothered, and now I was freezing cold and under attack from a whole colony of savage green ants.

The ferocity of the storm had swept them out of hibernation and into a delinquent frenzy all around me. This forced me to huddle for cover under a nearby tree. I was fully exposed to the elements, not because my shelter was saturated, but because I was getting my arse and face bitten by the carnivorous bastards.

Feeling like a dickhead, I sat there quivering in the rain with nothing to do but wait in wonder and try again tomorrow. There wasn't much left to think about sitting there in the darkness of the pelting rain, except for how much I hated ants.

I've gotta get out of here. Soon the sun would be up and then I wouldn't stop until I found the track back to the Boree intersection.

* * *

When the sun finally arrived, there were plenty of cow paddies lining the cow tracks for me to follow. But no cows, as usual.

I walked and walked. *Don't stop—it can't be that far.* How far did I have to keep walking to get out of here?

Finally my luck changed for the better and I arrived at what I assumed was the track I'd been searching for in the past two days. Unlike the cow tracks I'd been staggering in, the track to Boree was wide enough for a vehicle to travel along. It offered me some comfort at last.

It had to be important if there was a big sign painted in capital letters pointing to it. Surely people from the station either lived there or checked on it regularly.

I wasn't sure whether to turn back towards the intersection, or keep following the track further towards Boree. I settled on the latter to at least find out what it was, this place called

Boree. I figured it had to be the way. I must be getting closer to being saved.

Despite the hope of rescue again taking hold, I felt too buggered to keep going much further for the day, without knowing the consequences. To take my mind off the grinding sun rays, I threw myself into building a shelter, just off the edge of the track. This one would be more mozzie impenetrable than ever.

Knowing my luck, I thought a vehicle would probably run over me as I slept, but I didn't care. At least whoever was driving would probably stop to see what they hit.

Reverting back to the mud fortress formula, I reasoned that I didn't want to make the same mistake as the previous night. There was no way I was going to leave myself vulnerable to an ant invasion.

Digging the outline of a hole the length and width of me was tough going, due to the hardness of the ground. But I persisted in moulding mud slabs for my four walls until I could bury myself neatly inside.

It felt bigger and more comfortable than my previous effort. Measuring about 2 metres long and just wide enough inside for me to turn my head around, it was a huge improvement.

I spent hours smothering grass and branches over the compacted mud on top to try and make it mozzie-proof, but there is no such thing. Mosquitoes are very persistent. I escaped them for a little while, huddled in my dugout but, sure as shit, they came rattling through the walls eventually.

Gathering grass and cowshit to bury myself in was not an easy decision to make again. It hadn't worked too well before.

But there I was, all packed up in the shit in an attempt to deflect the insects, hoping for a decent night's sleep.

Having no food or fresh water was unbearable, but it wasn't the only horror about being stuck in the middle of nowhere. The mozzies made sure of that. Each day, my first and last thoughts were usually of how to evade those little black pricks.

* * *

The next morning, driven by my constant hunger, I decided to camp there another night to regain some strength. *I'll look for food, find some water, gather my thoughts and get moving.*

I wasn't having much success on the food front, but the early morning dew made the ground cold and moist. I grabbed my shirt again and dragged it through the grass, thoroughly sucking out the much-needed moisture in the hope it would cure my appetite as well.

After wringing the muddy drops into my mouth, I laid back on the vine I'd been using as a pillow and felt what I thought was a rock rubbing against my skull. Turning over to see what it was that felt so uncomfortable, I found what looked like a big juicy green mango hidden in the vine.

Where'd you come from, juicy bush mango? All that talking to God must have paid off.

Inside, the fruit contained a white fleshy substance; it had a bunch of bean sprouts springing from one end. It tasted delicious after so long without a decent feed. But there was only one of them staring back at me and I was left still feeling hungry after quickly devouring it.

Sitting there in the dirt next to my humpy, I saw a little brown lizard run past and—splat!—he's mine. I instinctively grabbed for him as soon as I saw him scampering past; I squashed his head with my right hand without really thinking of the consequences.

Sorry, little fella, I've got nothing against you personally, but I'm going to eat you. A bit of meat and veg to fend off the starvation.

He was pretty flattened by the impact and I had my doubts about his nutritional value. For the hell of it, I delicately peeled off his skin as best I could with my fingers. Being the first bit of meat to pass my lips since I'd been dumped, I wasn't going to feel too guilty about skinning his sorry arse.

But what was I supposed to do with him? Staring at my little lizard sitting on a piece of wood I found littering the ground, I had no idea how to best prepare him. My first thoughts were to cook him on the branch tenderly in the sun. But, after much contemplation, I opted to dry him out in the slight breeze and eat him raw for a quicker bite-sized meal.

I squeezed him with a purposeful grip of his back legs and dropped him down my gullet. He tasted delicious, stimulating my senses as he slithered down my throat.

Starting out with modest ideas of how to digest a little lizard, I soon progressed to ambitious dreams of lassoing a calf and tying it to a tree. I could use the vine I'd rolled up as a pillow to rope them up at my convenience. No worries.

Everything was fair game from then on, and that included me. I realised that any meal of substance I was going to have to chase down myself. Any creature that walked past had better be faster than me, or they were on the list.

For the rest of that day, I went searching through the surrounding scrub for food and found nothing. There wasn't even a decent patch of flowers to munch out on. *Surely I haven't eaten everything.* One piece of fruit and a smallish lizard couldn't be all that's out here.

That prospect put a huge dent in my already sinking spirits. I was slowly beginning to understand that all my determination might not pay off, no matter how dedicated I was to staying alive.

Lying there in the relative comfort of my humpy, my thoughts kept flashing back to the big blue-tongue lizard who had wandered past me on the road to the Boree intersection. *Why did I let him go?*

At that stage, I had been sure I wouldn't be stuck out there for any more than another day or two before a search party found me. I didn't think twice about watching big bluey get back to his own family. I encouraged him to keep plodding along.

Only later did the image stick in my head of how big and juicy he looked and how delicious he would've tasted. He must've weighed at least a few kilos; I was spewing I didn't eat him.

Trying to put big bluey into the back of my mind and to concentrate on the positives, I settled down for another night next to the track.

In the morning, I felt rested up and rejuvenated by a relatively peaceful night's sleep—a rarity for me. I hit the track hungry and thirsty, as usual. But I was better prepared from the rest and mentally fresh for the journey ahead.

I knew it would kill me if I didn't get moving again that day and find some food or water. I had to do whatever was required to prove my worth and will to survive.

If I had've known there was a dam waiting for me only a few kilometres further along the track, I wouldn't have bothered wasting two nights sleeping in the mud. But there was no harm done, and I marched on, as determined as ever.

9

DAM IT

While I had captured enough raindrops to stay alive and stumbled across the track to Boree again, the imminent threat of dehydration was constant. These cattle properties get pretty big, I reasoned, but the cows have to drink and so do I. There must be dams or waterholes out here somewhere.

After much contemplation, I figured that all the surface water that seeps into the ground had to go somewhere. Maybe it trickled down to the bottom of the hill. Too much rain had fallen for it all to disappear through the cracks, so where else could it go?

I followed the track for a few more kilometres, without result, until coming to rest beside a nice shady tree to sleep under, to avoid the hottest part of the day. As I sat there stunned by dehydration, I remembered an old Malcolm Douglas documentary I'd seen on TV years ago. Malcolm was one of those Bush Tucker Man types who knew all the survival tricks. Any tips I could remember would be well worth the effort.

On the program, he rambled on about a certain type of black rock being a sign there was water just below the surface. Looking down the track, I could see those same tiny pebble-like black rocks Malcolm had been blabbering about all those years ago. *Those black rocks over there, I've seen them before. There's water under them if I dig for it; that's what it said on that old TV show.*

It had something to do with the magnetic pull of the water to attract that type of rock, or so he reckoned. Figuring that Malcolm should know more about this stuff than me, I thought I might as well go and check out his bush survival theory for myself.

I got up from my resting spot and walked the few hundred metres to the bottom of the hill to have a go at digging through the dry clay. As sure as shit, I hit mud straight away. The old bastard was right!

Digging furiously in the crevices with my walking stick, I scraped deeper until striking muddy water. The deeper I dug, the cleaner was the water that pooled. Ripping into the ground like a well-oiled machine, I buried my face into the pool that was filling up and tried to filter out the mud with my teeth as best I could.

I couldn't help laughing at my new bush survival skill as I squatted there in the dirt like a blackfella. I replenished myself with what felt like litres of fresh water, until I felt ready to resume my hike.

There was nothing like a bit of rehydration, and the knowledge that Malcolm's plan actually worked, to put a spring in my step. After sucking enough fluids into me, I focused on finding the mother lode. A nice big healthy dam to feed the masses would be nice, thanks.

I was doing the right thing walking down the hill. *Follow the track and rely on your instinct, Rick—you've made it this far and you're still breathing.*

It was only about another kilometre down the track before the bush disappeared into an oversized paddock. There was a big green mound nestled in the distance and my mouth dropped in awe. *That's gotta be a dam.*

I could make out the outline almost as soon as I burst into the clearing. I couldn't believe it. Taking the shortest route possible through the potholes that littered the paddock, I satisfied my curiosity in the best way imaginable.

As I made my way closer, I realised that not only was it a dam, but one so full it was overflowing. I couldn't even follow the track anymore, the ground was that flooded. I thought I'd never have to drink my piss or pray for rain again.

About the only spot that remained dry was where I eventually built my humpy into the dam wall. I had to virtually swim across the paddock to get there.

Days of drinking stagnant water from filthy dugouts, combined with my chopped-up feet from all the walking, was all the convincing I needed to settle at the dam for a few days to recuperate. This plan was especially confirmed when I realised the dam was surrounded by all types of vegetation, some I'd never seen before. I could see frog holes and what looked like yabby tracks that pockmarked the dam wall and a good place for a dugout about halfway down. Unfortunately, I never did find any yabbies.

After a few hours of carving out the foundations of my humpy, I took off the rags I'd been using to soften the impact of the hard ground on my feet and finally allowed myself to relax. The water in the dam felt as fresh as if God had personally filled it Himself and I splashed around, swimming from bank to bank, looking for a fill of vegetation. The healthy amount of food lining the edge of the dam meant I could just slide up while flapping in the water and take a sample.

It was an amazing feeling to be floating in a full dam, surveying the huge amount of food at my fingertips. I felt like the king of a world in which no one else mattered.

Although I had only stumbled across the dam accidentally, I had immediate visions of the type of humpy I wanted to create. I felt like it was meant to be.

After splashing around for food and relaxation, I went back to my spot in the dam wall, facing west to catch the sunset. Digging away, I used my walking stick and scraped the dirt into the two strips of my t-shirt that had carried my aching feet so far, using them like the bucket of an excavator.

In my enthusiasm, I managed a hole around 1 metre deep by about 80 centimetres in diameter in just a few intensive hours. That was comfortable enough for my first night.

Once I hit that dam I met the big mamas of the mozzie kingdom. These ones were black and brown and boasted extra big wings that sounded just as evil as they appeared.

Those big girls rated a definite 5 Stars on the Bloody Hell barometer—for sure. I could hear them from metres away and they hunted in packs. They sounded like a plane approaching the darkened runway and hurt even before they'd sucked me dry and taken off full of my protein.

The dam also harboured a healthy team of minuscule brown mozzies. They didn't sting anywhere near as much as the rest of them—they were mild by comparison.

With these two new breeds mixed up with the other three types of mozzies I'd already met, it became intolerable. Up until then I could almost block them out if I really concentrated.

Swish, swish, swish. Their noise was so loud I thought I was going to get lifted up and carried away. Night-time was the time I really dreaded. They'd be in my ears, up my nose, on my eyelids—any fresh pieces of skin they could find, they latched on to.

In an attempt to protect myself, I dived inside the hole I'd dug into the dam wall and covered myself with my torn-up t-shirt.

The mozzies munched on me through the cotton, but my delight at having so much food and water at my disposal reduced the sense of aggravation. When that euphoria wore off, my master plan was for a protective shelter on a much grander scale.

My primary focus was to make a mozzie-proof home—that was not negotiable. Keeping dry and warm and out of the sun were my only other priorities. I sensed my luck had changed and revelled in the challenge of constructing a solid humpy I could feel proud to call home.

My walking stick marked out the structure in my humpy-building phases. I could measure the distances and prop up the mountains of dirt in the construction process with complete confidence.

The wear and tear led to a crack near the top of my trusty stick. Still, it never let me down and continued to work for my survival, despite its deterioration. I couldn't build a trench without it, cracked or not. There seemed to be no end to its versatility. Digging, sleeping, walking—I might even have used it as fuel if I could have lit a fire. Even if I had, it would still have probably come in handy for something afterwards, all charred up.

Thinking about extra uses for my stick also gave me ideas about the potential of my new environment. What else was lying around out there that might prove useful, if a bloody stick from the side of the track could be so handy?

I spotted a few star pickets on the edge of the paddock and scrambled over the few hundred metres to grab them. My walking stick had served me well as a digging tool up until then. But it couldn't compete with the reinforced strength of steel, especially a length that was sharpened at one end.

My humpy-building progress increased dramatically with the aid of my new weapons of penetration, along with my hopes of being found alive. For most of the heavy work, I used the star pickets and branches picked up from the perimeter of my new backyard.

I plodded away relentlessly; there was nothing better to do. I felt content with the knowledge that I seemed to be getting somewhere, finally.

Prisoners of war who tunnel their way to freedom were my inspiration. We shared the same desire to see the other side, no matter the obstacles. To me, it was clear that the big dam wall could form the backbone of an elaborate humpy of gigantic proportions.

My idea revolved around carving out a hole in the side of the dam wall that opened up into a big Yoda-type cave. I'd craft different rooms like an underground house someone would choose to live in.

I felt like the Diggers in Vietnam, churning into the side of the dam wall to camouflage my desperation. The impressive results gave me confidence that I could actually live comfortably out there after all, if I had to.

Every day, my sole emphasis was on improving my humpy. If I got hungry digging, there was a vegie patch at my feet. I had a swollen dam at my doorstep if I needed a refreshing dip.

I was constantly striving to increase my knowledge of how to construct a shelter that kept the mozzies out, and the warmth in. By making myself busy with this building phase, it took my mind off the fact I was fighting to survive.

For all the digging, my home essentially became one big circular underground chamber. I had to let go of my dream to have multiple rooms, to lessen the impossible maintenance. Still, my efforts were impressive. It didn't matter which way I spread myself across the floor, I had about 30 centimetres to spare at my head and my feet. If I sat upright inside, there was probably 30 centimetres of clearance to the roof as well.

To cover the entrance, I stuffed the hole with sticks and grass. The temperature was a good ten degrees warmer inside than out in the night air, and much cooler through the heat of the day. The insulation of the mud walls was as good as any commercial product you can buy from Bunnings.

I even managed to craft a pit toilet off to the side. It started out as a food shelf, but it collapsed in the rain as I slept one night. The crevice left behind by the deformed renovation formed a perfect round shape in the ground that grew as the walls deteriorated.

Each time I crawled in and out of my humpy, the crevice transformed into a more effective toilet basin. I could use it instead of letting the cold in whenever I had to crawl outside to relieve myself or take a shit.

Digging my humpy and collecting food provided my daily entertainment. There was so much new stuff to eat and I was that busy carving out my home, I had no time to worry about being rescued. I had plenty of food and water—it was just a matter of listening for cars or any sign of humans while I was digging.

To try and keep cool, I ripped the tattered bottoms off my shredding shorts and soaked them in water before wearing them as a hat. They had become annoying dangling so deteriorated below my thighs. At least by ripping off the denim and wetting them to put on my head, I could use them to cool down in the heat of the day.

Only when it rained did I run into trouble inside the relative safety of my cocoon. Whole chunks of hard dirt, ruptured by the pelting rain, would peel off my roof as my walls fell in on my head, and I huddled helplessly underneath. The force became so strong on a couple of occasions that all I could do was desperately head for the surface and catch my breath for fear of becoming permanently entombed.

Once I'd scrambled to the top, still half asleep, I then had to scoop out the mud that had smashed into me during the downpour and sleep in a depressing puddle. I knew that each time that occurred, most of the next day would consist of renovating the damage from the night before.

* * *

The paddymelons littering the ground summed up my situation pretty well. They were rough on the tastebuds but, with so many of them around, I knew I'd never go hungry. Unfortunately the one sour mouthful of paddymelon I did manage to digest left me feeling sick in the stomach. They looked edible, growing prosperously on the vines. But their rough yellowish skin hid the true extent of their foulness. I certainly didn't want to rely on them.

Little bugs offered a glimmer of hope, so I gave them a try. Then the crickets turned up and I sacrificed as many of them as I could fit in my mouth.

Crickets were the first really crunchy thing that I tried, but definitely not the last. They made a nice change from the softness of the mushy vegetation I'd become accustomed to. Being so small and crunchy, all the unlucky munchkins I could grab hold of I swallowed whole. I pulled off their heads and chewed the rest down as fast as I could, so I didn't have to dwell on what I was actually eating.

Grasshoppers were pretty crunchy as well. I didn't really appreciate the sensation of the legs and wings tickling the insides of my cheeks—they were too spindly for my liking. To counter that, I pulled off their limbs and just ate the body, which made them more palatable.

Adopting that method, I happily included them on the growing list of appetisers. After noticing how plentiful they were around the dam, they were a welcome distraction from all the sizeable animals that seemed to be avoiding me so successfully.

Not bad, not bad at all, and they tasted better by the growing handful. They had a bit more flavour and were a bit meatier than crickets, even minus the arms and legs. More fulfilling and easier to digest.

Both insects twisted around plenty if I didn't swallow fast. They never went out without a struggle, but the end result was always the same. To me the crickets and grasshoppers were dead once I pulled their heads off, but they weren't so easily convinced. They wriggled around in my mouth until my teeth crushed their brittle bodies into bite-sized pieces.

Some people may wince at the thought of eating crickets and grasshoppers, but they really are quite all right. Close your eyes and pray to God, and you'd be surprised what you can stomach. I didn't plan to eat so many of them, but there's not a lot of choice when you're starving in the desert. It was grasshoppers or grass. I knew which alternative I preferred.

Having a crack at any type of food that didn't look or smell like it could kill me had become my motto for survival. Leeches were one of those creatures I didn't expect to go down so smooth. I'd eat one of them again any day, and track down his mates for seconds. For anyone who hasn't tried leeches, they are some of the sweetest tucker you're ever likely to find when lost in the outback. I'd heartily recommend them, as long as you learn how to chew fast.

I wasn't sure what to expect when the first leech went down—they kind of snuck up on me as a delicacy. In the desert of all places, I wasn't counting on finding any, but they quickly rose up the ranks and became elevated to a position near the top of the food chain.

They imagined they were coming to me to feed on me, when I was flapping about in the dam to get their attention. They seemed oblivious to where all the other leeches in the dam had disappeared to. It was pretty easy to attract them.

But, just like the crickets and grasshoppers, they didn't give up so easily. I had to remember to chomp my gums fast, or they'd plant their suckers onto the inside of my cheek for a feed of their own.

I was tongue-sucked by the leeches on a few occasions, but that only spurred me on to bite back twice as hard. I wouldn't tolerate any argument about who was having who for dinner. When everything went according to plan, the leeches slithered straight down my throat and I was left with the same sense of satisfaction I had previously bestowed on unlucky lizards.

These leeches were as thick as my middle finger. Really big and juicy suckers. They were a bit tough and squishy in texture because they were so fat, but extremely delicious nonetheless.

Smart leeches, dumb leeches, fat leeches, skinny ones—they all dropped by to say hello eventually. All I had to do was lie back in the water and flap about, waiting for the little squirmies to arrive. Their dinner plans became my dinner plans, until they all disappeared.

Just like finding water, or fending off the multitude of mozzies, sorting out food emerged as one of the perennial problems to solve. I could waste dozens of hours chasing scraps for no result, or it could just fall into my lap as if I had a fork in my hand.

One decent meal that landed on me when I least expected it occurred when I noticed the crab holes etched into the mud wall. I originally thought they must have been frog holes. Fine by me—I liked frogs.

I jabbed a stick down the hole to find out for sure, when something lashed out and grabbed hold. I saw his little crabby face poking up from the blackness and coaxed him out of there for a closer look. Soon enough, he and his family were being added to my growing menu.

Crabs are pretty stupid, I came to realise. Every time one of them thought there was something causing a commotion on top of his house, he came out to muscle up for a fight. Then I ate him.

I almost felt sorry for them vanishing so rapidly from the dam without a trace. But they tasted too good to get emotional over or to slow down on their slaughter.

Without a fire or anything to cook on, I just cracked the shells there and then and ripped into the delicious meat. They tasted better than any meal I've ever eaten at a fancy restaurant, plus I didn't have to leave a tip.

In the end I coaxed out from their hidey holes six or seven crabs about the size of the palm of my hand. I ate what I reckoned was a fair chunk of the dam's entire crab population. They were the only crustaceans I came across in my days floundering around at that dam anyway. And, fuelled by my selfish appetite, I checked out pretty much everywhere.

10

FEAST OR FAMINE

It was proving hard to get a balanced diet relying entirely on what nature could provide. It was feast or famine, depending on the state of the surrounding environment.

Meat of any description was the substance I craved; I was prepared to do whatever was required. But without that opportunity of a carnivorous feast always available to me, I sure ate a lot of vegetation. Edible plants didn't stand a chance with me around.

One type of vegetation I christened 'bopples' became my staple food source. They were there for me more than any other type of vegetation and settled quite nicely on the palate. By the time I found my first patch of bopples, I'd eaten so many shit foods already I was just hoping they tasted half decent.

From my first mouthful I found they had a bit more flavour than the other types of vegetation I'd been forced to endure. Little bopples especially became something to search out on my food runs. They tasted similar to little snow peas fresh out of the pod. All I had to do to get my fill was peel back the outside like a banana and pop the balls of goodness into my mouth.

Once I peeled back the outer green crust, they appeared like garden peas—as if they were growing in my very own vegetable garden. It looked like there was nothing inside the succulent bopple pods—but, sure enough, there were little green balls that shot out. I just had to squeeze below the purple flowers that identified them. As an extra treat, the bopples also harboured dry stringy stalks, which branched out and which I could suck on.

The bopple bushes varied greatly in size. The smaller ones were just tiny shrubs that didn't measure much higher than my shins. But after a decent dose of rain—or in certain patches that sprang up randomly—they could grow to chest height.

When I initially found the bopples sprouting, I pulled the branches from the bushes and ate the stem as well. A good stem stretched about as thick as the handle of a pool cue and tasted a bit like a slushy piece of wood, which was hardly bearable. But they were a desirable addition to the menu when food was at a premium.

The bigger bopples were a bit huskier inside. Although they were much bigger, the fruits of those big bushes sacrificed their taste with their hollowness from becoming so sun-dried.

Also, when I cracked them open, they were more likely to have holes from the caterpillars and ants invading them. That made the bigger bopples less attractive, plus I didn't have to peel the little ones.

I soon gave up on picking the stems as an alternative food source, with so many wholesome bopple bushes to consume. Why bother sucking on the slops if the good stuff was so plentiful?

After about the fourth or fifth day at the dam, it rained and the bopples started to really sprout. They doubled in size overnight and the delectable pods poked out at me ripe for the picking. If I was lucky, I'd find a couple of juicy grasshoppers burrowing into the bigger bopples to wash the whole meal down with. That would cover just about all the food groups in the one sitting.

'Spriggie-spriggies' were the bush tucker bean sprouts I first found growing at the bottom of my humpy. Once I spotted that first bunch, I looked around the fringes and could see them springing up everywhere. They were glistening green pods baking in the sun, and they rested among more delicious bopples than I could hope to poke a stick at.

Wild radish roots were something else to add to my growing menu. They were nothing flash, but again they filled a hole. The wild radishes grew around the edge of the dam. They looked and tasted like radishes, hence the name I gave them.

My wild radish roots were anchored firmly in the soil and grew flat along the ground. The bush vegies poked out from the bundles of green leaves that enveloped them—I had to pull them up from the ground like a vine.

Pasta would be a good meal to throw wild radish roots into. Spriggie-spriggies would probably be best served to complement a lasagne. Bopples seemed ideal to grind into a paste to make a sauce or a dip.

Bopples always remained a favourite, though. I imagined the flavour they produced and what I could do with them after I was found alive. Big Rick's Bopple Jam—it was something I thought would be so delicious, it would make Paul Newman's efforts to cash in on the pasta sauce market appear pathetic.

In my enthusiasm to discover new dishes, I kept alive the dream of getting out of there and eating a proper meal. Perhaps I could complement those first few mouthfuls with new delicacies!

The mozzies were not to escape the menu either. With so many swarms to contend with, it seemed my only hope in the impending madness. I looked down under a bright February moon to see my arms and legs completely covered in thousands of mozzies. Each one was fighting for a spot on my quickly disappearing skin.

It didn't matter how many of them I bludgeoned, all I managed was to cover myself in more blood and mozzie bites for the victims' relatives to feast on.

I did eat a couple of mozzies. They tasted like flies—which was okay to me—but I started to dwell on the possibility of contracting Ross River fever. How fucked would that be? They were bad enough biting me, I reckoned I shouldn't be eating them at all.

* * *

As I began to settle in for an early night about five days after I'd arrived at the dam, I suddenly heard the unmistakable rumble of a Harley-Davidson motorbike—I'd know that sound anywhere. Climbing out of my humpy, I tried to pick up the source of the rumbling so I could go in search of its headlights.

Over the previous few days, I'd watched helplessly as another plane far on the horizon conducted what I assumed was its regular mail run. Such planes were no bigger than specks in the far distance, maybe 50 kilometres away as the crow flies. However, I was determined not to let the rumble of the Harley escape me so easily.

I couldn't see anything from ground level, but I could certainly hear it. Desperate to trace the distinctive sound of the motorbike, I ran frantically through the paddock in search of higher ground.

Who knows how long I ran for? It felt like a few minutes, but it could have been hours. The sound became fainter with each passing step and my mind was frantic. I couldn't even be sure I hadn't imagined the whole thing.

When I finally reached the top of a nearby hill, I couldn't see anything through the canopy of trees. Out of frustration, I climbed the tallest gum tree I could find in the hope I might catch a glimpse of those elusive headlights. But there was nothing. All that running had left me exhausted and I had nothing to show for it.

By then I felt too buggered to stagger all the way back to my humpy and anyhow, I wasn't capable of figuring out in which direction I needed to go to head home in the darkness. I decided to catch some sleep away from the mozzies by staying up the tree and clinging to its branches.

To give myself more stability, I climbed down to a solid fork and wrapped my arms around the tree trunk. The wind whipped the leaves violently and the mozzies kept nagging at me, but I was determined to ignore them both. I closed my eyes on all my troubles, hoping it was all just a bad dream.

In the morning, reality reminded me quick smart that I was in big trouble. I scrambled back up to the top branches to get a better view of my surroundings. Scanning the paddocks, I could see no trace of my dam. I wasn't even sure in which direction to go. Once again, I found myself vulnerable to the elements. I had no water and no idea.

I couldn't believe I'd risked sleeping so high up the tree to minimise the impact of mozzies. One slip and I would've been nursing fractured bones for sure. That would have guaranteed my demise.

Angry for leaving myself so open to broken bones and dehydration again, I clambered down to the ground, found some cow tracks and started the familiar march to nowhere. But, just when all hope appeared lost, some thriving ponds full of waterlilies appeared through the bushes. It was the first time I'd ever stumbled across this succulent delicacy.

Waterlilies were another real treasure. They had a watermelon-like texture and tasted similar to alfalfa. The combination of moisture and vegetation in the same mouthful worked an absolute treat. All I had to do was pull the leaves off, about two inches from the top of the plant's stem, and I could suck on the rest. It tasted like a spriggie-spriggie ice-block.

Rejuvenated, I managed to find a track leading back to the dam without too much further trouble. And I vowed never to leave my dam in the shadows of darkness again.

* * *

It didn't rain much at the dam, just the odd downpour, but then again, with such a plentiful water supply, I didn't really need it to. Sometimes I could see the rain clouds forming in the distance, but they generally skirted past without making a deposit.

With not much rain falling, though, the dam's water level dropped sharply and my previously jubilant mood dipped with it. The big picture of me still being stranded re-emerged.

I couldn't go to the shops, or get a drink from the kitchen tap. I still had to work for everything I had and seemed to be getting no closer to being rescued. It was getting drier and drier and the channels of water that had saturated the paddock when I found the dam returned to dirt.

The cycles in the desert of the times when it rained and the times when it didn't continually perplexed me. But, as long as I kept making good decisions, I felt confident I could make it out alive.

One of the toughest of those decisions I had to face during my lone incarceration was when I should abandon my reliable water source at the dam. It was something I wrestled with for days before acting on it.

I reasoned that, if I sat there and waited for things to happen, I was bound to die. Even if I made a wrong choice in moving on, at least it would keep my mind ticking over. I could devise another plan to get out of whatever new misadventure I'd created for myself.

Frustration started to creep in and that bred desperation. Apart from the lack of cows at the dam, the sound of planes in the far distance was also really pissing me off. I had some food and water, but the reality remained the same. I was still stuck in the middle of nowhere and no closer to getting out alive.

My brain and my body both knew I had to get off my arse and find a better view of those planes I kept hearing. But each day seemed a constant battle to get my mind, body and spirit in synch. One day I'd think of heading off, but my body wouldn't feel energised enough. The next morning my body felt ready to go, but my mind and spirit weren't interested. Either way, I couldn't muster the motivation to walk off into the unknown.

It was like having four or five different personalities inside me, with each one pulling in a different direction. In the wash-up, I decided my options were clear. Either I put in one more attempt at trying to walk out and find someone while I still had the strength, or I would sit helpless in my hole in the dam wall and hope those planes in the distance ultimately noticed me.

I'd made a big effort to try and put on a bit of weight by eating virtually anything I could get my hands on in the eight days since I'd been at the dam. The rest had done my feet some good as well.

Finally, the infuriating sight and sound of the distant planes had become too much. Combined with the strength I'd built up from having a constant supply of food, water and rest, it spurred me on to set out on one final bid for freedom.

I tried to collect enough vegetation to keep me going for a few days. Packing pockets full of bopples and spriggie-spriggies and tying as many waterlilies as I could fit around my waist, I was good to go.

Surely there were other waterholes further along the track filled with crabs and leeches. There were none left in my dam and they tasted so delicious.

Leaving behind a humpy I'd put so much blood, sweat and tears into constructing haunted me. But it had to be done to improve my chances of being found alive.

At least I felt sure the experience gained from putting in so much effort to build such a comfortable temporary home would prove invaluable for future protective designs. With that in mind, I reluctantly climbed out of my hole for the last time and began what I hoped would be my final food run.

As usual, I woke up not long after sunrise. I was reluctant in both body and mind to pursue my departure, but knew I had to overcome these fears to survive. It took until well into mid morning before I felt capable of carrying through my intention.

I had no cup or anything to carry water with me, so I was well aware I could find myself in trouble pretty quickly if the track to Boree was bone dry. Much to my disappointment, I could find no water once I marched off. Nothing except for a couple of little waterholes within the first few hundred metres, where I stopped to munch out on a welcome patch of waterlilies.

The only other moisture I could capture was by dragging my t-shirt through the grass, but that was hardly substantial. They were drops rather than mouthfuls. I made slow progress and, almost as soon as I started walking, I had to sit down again for a rest.

I felt like my legs had the stamina to carry me as far as I needed to go, but they just couldn't carry my sagging weight.

Having the sun beating down on me didn't help—it sapped all my energy. I could feel the rays ripping right through me. Like a steak left on the barbie, I was well done. It was too hot to bear any longer and I latched onto the welcome shelter of a small tree.

I reckoned I'd get further by walking at night, out of the sun. With that in mind, I decided to sit in the shade until after dusk and then put in a big effort.

In the cooler weather of the night, I found I could muster about a kilometre at a time without stopping. But by about midnight, I was stuffed and couldn't go any further. By then I'd gobbled up most of my food stash and didn't seem any closer to anywhere. With nothing else to do, I looked around for somewhere comfortable to sleep. I knew the sun was coming up in five or six hours and had a feeling it was going to be another blistering hot day.

It's depressing how well you can predict the weather for the next morning in the middle of the night, once you get used to it. Unless I got some rest, I'd find myself collapsing as soon as the sun began to bite.

There was a lot of grass on the side of the track and I devised a plan to use it to my advantage. Who knows how long I spent in the process of making my primitive camp? I just rolled and rolled around in the long grass until I resembled a gigantic ball of fluff so thick that I couldn't see my hand in front of my face. The stacks of grass locked together like glue.

On the plus side it was nice and toasty inside, and I didn't smell like shit as I'd expected. It felt a bit eerie though, sleeping there like a rolled-up haystack. I sensed a cow or a dingo creep around my grass monster during the night, but I ignored this distraction. And despite hearing the rain pelt down at one stage, I woke up as dry as a hotel pillow.

As daylight slowly dawned, it came with all the intensity of a bad morning in hell. When I climbed out of my cocoon, I was pretty shocked to see in the harshness of that light the size of the ball I'd created. I knew I'd gathered up a lot of grass the night before, but the huge bare patch surrounding me came as a surprise.

I'd pulled out the strands of grass in a clockwise direction as I rolled around collecting them and the pattern it created looked puzzling. If someone had happened to fly over me they'd think the gigantic circular-shaped remnants I'd left in my wake were a sign of aliens for sure. Maybe they'd even contact the authorities; that could only be a good thing.

That day was one of the hottest I can remember during my whole time in the desert. I'm not sure if my exhaustion magnified the intensity of the sun's rays, but I couldn't even concentrate on the next step ahead of me, let alone plan how to get out of the dire predicament I'd put myself in.

Maybe this would be my last gamble. I'd rolled the dice once too often and for that I was about to pay the ultimate penalty. After just a couple of hours, I could feel myself weakening to a pitiful state. I was taking smaller steps and stopping for longer rests more often.

I cursed myself for becoming so exposed to dehydration again and felt unsure about how I was ever going to make it. I had to keep shuffling along the winding track I'd been following. *You've gone too far to turn back, Rick, and there might be a clearing up ahead. You can make another stint—get over it.*

Just when I felt at my most vulnerable, I emerged from the tree line to see what I hoped was my ultimate salvation—a massive paddock full of brown grass and a pyramid-shaped green mound on the horizon.

If that's what I think it is, I'm saved. If it's not, then I'm pretty well fucked. My mind was made up that this green mountain was my only hope. I'd gone almost a day without a drop of water and my throat was closing up.

It didn't look that far to get to. I figured it couldn't be more than a kilometre away and then I'd have a nice big gulp of fresh water for all my troubles. But it was one thing to see the big green mound and another challenge entirely to harness the energy to get there. I was completely buggered and couldn't work out how I would make the distance without any moisture to sustain me in the baking heat.

For an entree, I stumbled on some delectable little purple flowers poking out of the grass. They were like snow peas in a sea of muck. Christening them 'schnurples' for their colour, I was amazed to discover they held small sachets of water collected from the morning dew. They were good for a couple of satisfying slurps, that was for sure.

These schnurples were bell-shaped flowers that grew on a vine; they were bursting with moisture and I gladly lapped them up. There was only a tiny amount of water in each flower, but every drop invigorated my soul and I picked them carefully so as not to spill any.

A few times I was a bit heavy-handed and paid the price with a spillage. For the most part, however, their delicate contents made their way to my cracked lips. But I still spat the dummy whenever I did spill one, cursing myself for my clumsiness.

Fucking idiot! Concentrate or perish.

I was simultaneously sucking flowers to survive and salivating at the prospect of a dam in the far distance. But even with a few sips of water to sustain me, I could only manage short hikes before needing a rest. Only later, after I was rescued, did I learn that my schnurples were a sign that delectable yams were hidden in the ground underneath. Another food source that escaped me because I didn't know where to look.

I didn't want to sit down for too long—that only made it harder to get going again. Plus I couldn't handle the suspense.

Hoping against all hope that it was a dam, I prayed to God. *I'll beg if You want me to!* There was no other reason for a big green mound to appear across the paddock; it had to have water in it. Dam or no dam, I wasn't going to make it any further. I'd lost too much energy to keep searching. Someone was going to have to find me on its banks, or else that big green mound would become my gravesite. This had to be that Boree place.

Crossing the paddock towards the big green mound, there were more grass splinters to contend with. The soles of my feet had become my own personal splinter factory. The ground looked soft, but the grass felt uncomfortably razor sharp. I could feel shards digging into my toes with surgical precision, working their way deeper and deeper into my flesh until I picked them out or fell over.

The sun was burning my face and lips—even the tops of my hands were getting torched. I was becoming more frustrated with all the walking. I didn't seem to be getting any closer to the green mountain, which always looked the same distance away.

Eventually I had to tell myself, *Rick, just don't look at it. You'll get there quicker. Stop being a girl and don't look up!* But I'd still sneak little glimpses when I didn't think anyone was looking. Each step was a marathon effort—I passed out face first into the ground a few times.

In my dazed state, I was having more visions of my ex-girlfriend Julie calling out to me: 'Come on, baby, you can't sleep here. It's time to go. Keep going—get up!'

My eyes narrowed halfway across the field. I felt like I had a purpose but I didn't seem to have the energy required to get there. Just lifting my head up left me feeling dizzy and I fell over again. All I could manage, with about 800 metres to go, was to get up on my knees and drag myself along with my walking stick to support my weight.

As I clawed to within a few hundred metres, the big green mound multiplied. I could make out not just one big grassy knoll, but two other smaller parcels on either side.

My mind started playing tricks on me. Maybe this wasn't a dam at all. Maybe I'd used up all this energy to chase something that didn't exist. *These could be your last moments, Rick—what are you going to think about?*

The big green mountain was topped with grass, which looked so soft and velvety. I thought: *even if it isn't a dam, at least I'll die on a nice soft hill.* A more tolerable death, if I could make it that far.

There was no point dwelling on whether I should have gone this way or taken that turn. I had not an ounce of strength left to argue with myself. Although I was ready to die, I didn't want to after all I'd been through and having reached this far. I wanted another crack at living and felt I'd done enough to deserve it.

Centimetre by centimetre, I crawled towards my big green mountain. Each grassy patch I crawled across, hand over foot, brought me closer to the realisation I might be right.

At last, I caught my first glimpse of the liquid gold seeping out of the big green mound. An awe-inspiring feeling overwhelmed me. Not only was it a dam, and a fairly big dam at that, but it also had two overflow dams lapping either side. There was so much water I didn't know what to do with it all. Or so I thought.

Crawling to the edge of the first overflow, I grabbed handfuls of bopples to shove in my mouth. I even began filling my pockets, in case they all mysteriously disappeared. The overflow might have been brown and muddy, but it was still a sight for sore eyes and I gleefully rolled into it.

Mud became muddy water, which became water with a bit of mud in it. I was so thirsty and appreciative, I didn't care about the filthy content.

There was one overflow dam in the foreground and another one just behind the main dam, separated only by a few metres of sloshy channels. After I caught my breath, the big green mound called out to me like a lush oasis. It was now less than a hundred metres away, and I shuddered with expectation. For the first time in days, I felt like I was going to be found alive. It could be today, or it could be tomorrow, but someone would surely discover me.

I couldn't picture running out of food, or losing more than half my body weight. I certainly never considered that after twenty-odd days already spent wandering the desert I'd have to wait another seven weeks to be found. In many respects my fight for survival had in fact only just begun.

11

THE BIG GREEN MOUND

Climbing up to the top of the big green mound, fresh from wallowing in the overflow, I discovered a magnificent pool of sustenance of gigantic proportions. I wasted no time at all sinking into its swollen belly, laughing myself silly at the blessing that the water tasted even fresher than it looked.

For a man on the brink of death, it was as if I was drinking from God's own water source. It was like it had been poured down from the heavens, just for me. *Lap it up, Rick, you need it.*

The realisation I was still alive slowly washed over me with a feeling of overwhelming relief. If it hadn't turned out to be a dam, there was simply no way I could have kept going. To be swimming in a thriving pool, filled to the brim with the clearest water I'd ever tasted, was purely astonishing.

Rich green grass lined the dam bed and I grabbed fistfuls as I splashed around. I sucked them so furiously, to extract whatever nourishment they contained, that the fine edge of the grass blades sliced my lips open.

Not that I really cared about the bleeding. The nourishing sensation cleansed the pores of my skin and stimulated my soul completely.

The landscape seemed just as beautiful as the thriving dam. There were acres of vegetation lined by large shady trees to provide a welcome canopy from the harsh sunlight.

It was hard to imagine that, just a few minutes earlier, I'd been dragging my sorry arse through this same paddock, ready to give up on seeing the day out. All of a sudden my days weren't numbered after all.

Sitting up there on my grassy knoll, it felt like I'd crawled into a mini-oasis. I'd inherited my own patch of paradise in the desert.

Nearby were some cattle yards. That indicated that someone, at some time, must come and check on what appeared to be a mustering point for the station. Regardless of when that moment arrived, I had heaps of food at my disposal and no shortage of water.

There were green frogs jumping around everywhere. The bopple bushes grew as big as small trees and fed the platoon of grasshoppers. What else could a starving man ask for?

As I sat there soaking it all in, sucking back a few flavoursome bopples, I spotted a large water monitor swaggering towards the dam. He would have measured about 2 metres in length and appeared very cautious as he slipped in to cool off, just as I'd done an hour or so earlier.

With an air of confidence I'd been missing since being dumped and left for dead, I gave him a nod. *You're gonna be mine soon, sucker!*

Watching him bob up and down in the water without a worry in the world just made me want to eat him all the more. But I was content for the time being to sit back as a passive observer. If he got used to me being around, he would be that much easier to catch down the track.

Cows were mooing in the distance and I began to moo in reply. I was hoping they'd come over and check me out. I still had my vine with me that I'd collected along the track to the first dam; maybe I could lasso one for lunch. Unfortunately, my moos weren't as convincing as I thought and that was the last I heard or saw of any bovines.

I acknowledged out loud for the first time that I wouldn't mind seeing Julie and my family again for real—I could make it. It had to be God who was making these things happen for me.

To repay the favour, I committed myself to whatever path He wanted me to follow. I opened up the line of communication, ready to accept any orders He thought necessary. *God, if You want me to change my ways, then just let me know. Whatever it is You want, it will be done. I stand here as Your disciple prepared to give myself up for You, without questioning the reasons for Your decisions.*

While we never made any promises to each other, we seemed to have an understanding. He knew that if He wanted me to go out there and do good in the community, become a priest or whatever, He just had to let me know. I would obey His every order.

I told Him I was there waiting to find out what it was He wanted from me, but He refused to say. Somehow I was meant to work it out for myself.

Still, He was doing enough to keep me living and breathing. When I prayed in moments of utter desperation, something would always happen to help me through whatever nightmare was confronting me. I couldn't explain it, but that's how things were between us.

I estimated there was enough vegetation at my fingertips to last me another six months. I felt certain that this was where I'd be rescued, probably sooner rather than later.

After regaining some strength with a gutful of food and water, I went to work on building what I hoped would become my ultimate shelter. My grand plans were of building a real fair-dinkum house, made out of solid timber right next to the dam. I wanted a home like the one in *Little House on the Prairie*. I'd construct it out of timber sourced from the tall trees that were only a stone's throw away on the edge of the paddock.

If a pilot couldn't see me sitting on the bank of the dam, then surely they'd notice a complete house perched on the edge that hadn't existed before. Plus, I wasn't sure how much longer I'd be stuck out there. I wanted to live out the remainder of my days in the desert in a degree of comfort normally reserved for those who actually resided on the station.

My eyes were bulging at the opportunities. I envisioned crafting a chopping tool from the bits and pieces of fencing materials that surrounded the dam. That way I could retrieve the timber required to construct my extravagant five-star log cabin. I'd have several rooms. Maybe a fireplace to keep warm at night, and definitely a cooking pit dug in the ground to prepare meals of substance. Panoramic views from the encircling verandah would complete the picture. I could even knock up a few rough bits of furniture if I had the time; something to leave behind as a legacy when I was returned to civilisation.

Unfortunately, not even my sincerest resourcefulness stretched to this extent. Transforming a star picket and a piece of fencing wire into a lethal weapon, sharp enough to fell solid wood up to a foot in diameter, proved far beyond my capabilities.

Instead of chopping down the trees, I tried to come up with a more realistic tree-plundering method. Maybe I could pull down and snap off the big branches and drag them back to the dam, using brute strength and my piece of vine to rope them in.

After several attempts to lasso my lumber, it became obvious I'd require the muscles and skill of a lumberjack to undertake this task. Unfortunately, I just didn't have that in me. Once again, my pathetic physical condition meant I was too weak for the job. I had to admit defeat.

The log cabin was a nice dream, but the reality was I'd have to make do with something more modest. In retrospect, I felt my homestead dream had been a stupid proposition and it only served to frustrate me even further.

In the meantime, the feed trough I'd spotted as I'd crawled up the dam bank seemed a viable short-term option. It appeared that when the main dam overflowed, the converted feed trough acted as a guide to channel the water into the overflow dam below. I figured it should keep me dry for a few nights and sort out the mozzies.

It was a bloody big unit. By the feel of it, I guessed it weighed 80 kilograms and measured more than 2 metres in length. After dismantling the pump set-up, I spent the best part of the next hour trying to drag the trough up to the top of the grassy mound. I decided that was the best place to build my new humpy.

It took all my energy to drag it the ten or so metres I needed to move it. I had no strength left in my arms and my legs had turned to jelly.

In normal circumstances, I would've just thrown the trough over my shoulder like a slab of cold beer in seconds. Instead, in my weakened state, I had to improvise by harnessing all my strength to stand it upright. Then I used my weight to pull it back towards me, end over end.

If I didn't jump out of the way in time, the trough would slam me into the ground. My efforts would have been comical if their purpose wasn't so important. But after a good hour and a few bruises for my troubles, I finally had somewhere to sleep. I had achieved another milestone.

* * *

While the volume of vegetation impressed me from the start, I was hoping for a few more crabs and leeches to play with. But sadly, there were no crabs at all in that dam. It did harbour leeches, but not nearly as many as I expected given its comparatively imposing size.

Crabs and leeches were my two favourite foods when roughing it. I never really thought of frogs much, until one jumped out in front of me. But they ended up being pretty irresistible as well.

My first green frog I found sitting on the edge of the main dam. I watched him for a few minutes and he didn't move.

He just sat there, oblivious to my greedy intentions, until I snuck up and put him out of his misery.

I looked over the other side of the dam and there were frogs of all descriptions hopping about. That gave me the energy to get amongst them for a real feast.

I had earlier discovered a tin near the pump and it became one of my prized possessions. The broken-down water pump was hidden behind the dams next to some cattle yards about 200 metres from my humpy and harboured a collection of odds and ends used to mend and maintain it.

Armed with my new tin I could use for drinking, I began a daily ritual of collecting frogs in it. My attempts fluctuated between flourishing and pathetic, depending on my luck and appetite.

Early in the morning was the best time to catch them. I'd lie in my humpy waiting for the right moment—just after sunrise—to go frog hunting. It quickly became my favourite time of the day.

If I snuck up on them expertly, I could have a handful of them for a wholesome breakfast in a matter of minutes. Too slow and it was back to bopples.

At first I had tried to peel off their skins, but that was pretty hard going, particularly if they were large, and it didn't make a huge difference to the overall taste.

Sitting on the edge of my upturned tin trough, scanning for juicy frogs, I had one of those Einstein moments. The sun was pretty extreme, as usual, banging away like the bad songs I couldn't get out of my head. The light bulb flashed above me and my mind started ticking over. If the trough burnt my bum after just a few hours of sunlight, imagine what I could cook on it through the heat of a whole day.

Continuing with this theory, I shaped some pieces of wire I'd collected from the nearby fence into skewers. I threaded a frog onto one piece of wire, making sure he was stitched up good enough so he couldn't hop away. The metal was that hot, my little frog sizzled almost the instant I threw him on the scorching surface. Instant frog kebabs—a real treat for meat lovers!

I was soon having wild ideas about what else I could cook up on my bush barbie. Goannas, kangaroos, cows—there were no limits to what I could burn on this baby. I'd be eating well, however long I was stuck out there.

If anything, my hot trough method proved too effective at frying my culinary delights. They shrivelled up in minutes if I became distracted and forgot I'd slapped a serving onto my barbie.

Birds became my nemesis. I now realised I wasn't losing my mind—the frogs I had left simmering on the stove weren't vanishing into thin air, but were disappearing into the stomachs of those flying food thieves.

I lost a few frogs to self-preservation as well. Somehow, a few of them managed to pull themselves off the skewer and limp away. That meant I had to either go without, or crawl around on the ground to locate and rewire them. Still, it was generally an effective method to create munchable delicacies.

When I did lose a healthy-looking specimen, I'd get pretty pissed off. It didn't matter how good or bad I was going with my food collecting, a frog was still a frog. I caught them fair and square, with my own bare hands, and deserved the spoils. If I really thought about it, they escaped fair and square as well, so we could both win and lose.

The brown frogs were a lot harder to catch than the green ones, but much more satisfying in my stomach. They were a bit smaller than their slimy green cousins. Lightning quick off the mark and super cunning when I tried to ambush them, but they were definitely more delicious. They tasted much sweeter and I could eat them whole.

The green ones I had to gut and dry out to digest. They still tasted fresh and tangy, as long as I didn't eat the intestines. With smaller front legs than the brown variety, they had enough nice fleshy meat tucked around the body to compensate.

I ran my wire straight through the middle and pulled their guts out; I opened their mouths to scoop the meat out with my fingers. It was a strange taste to begin with, but one I relished for its nourishment value. I sometimes added a few gum leaves to spice them up if I felt really inspired and wanted to enhance the flavour.

Brown or green, frogs were meatier than most other things I was shoving down my throat. They grew to a reasonable size too, so they received a big thumbs up.

One frog I regret eating was the big green fella whose glory days were well past him. In truth, he caught me more than the other way around. I just looked around me when I was on a food run one afternoon out in the paddock; at that moment, he glanced up at me sadly and started to hobble off.

You're gone, buddy! The big fella was on a piece of wire I always carried with me before he had time to swallow his own dinner. He reinforced my theory that some days I had to fight for a feed, while at other times my meals basically committed suicide before my eyes.

On a better hunting expedition, I probably would have let him go. He looked so sickly—a real off-green colour—but I was in no position to be choosey. I took him back to my place for a cook-up. That big, fat, old green frog didn't look much healthier than me. But there were so few of them around by then, I sent him down the food chute anyway.

He tasted as wrong as he looked and left me feeling off-green as well. He was one sick motherfucker I reckon I did a favour by skewering. After just a couple of mouthfuls, I threw him out for the ants to gorge themselves sick on. I paid the price for my own greed with a hell of a gut-ache.

* * *

My new home was kind of shaped like a thinly squeezed igloo—a cattle trough turned upside down like a bath with the ends chopped off to create shelter. It was comfortable enough on the inside, despite the fact that I was unable to turn around in it. But it was far from mozzie-proof. I had to go for a swim first thing most mornings to wash all the mozzie guts off me and rub some mud into the bites.

To try to deter the mozzies, I hung the two halves of my battered t-shirt—the rags I'd carried all those miles to nurse my chopped-up feet—at either end of the trough. They acted as curtains when shut tight.

One half of my old shirt did the job perfectly, but the other end of my humpy was only partially covered because that half of my shirt was smaller. To give me better protection,

I packed the exposed corner with mud and leaves, and hoped for the best.

It didn't matter how much grass I shoved into each end to plug up the spaces left around my shirt curtains, the mozzies still managed to wriggle underneath the trough. They didn't miss a beat.

No mozzie swarms could penetrate the trough's metal exterior. But I was still stuck with the ones trapped inside, the ones who lived and bred in the grass beneath me. They certainly knew where to go for a feed.

At least it wasn't the mozzie stampede I'd previously grown accustomed to. I could see and hear and swat most of them as they sucked me dry. But they still drove me crazy enough with their persistence, so much so that I relocated my humpy further down the dam bank to try and find relief.

The result was always the same, though. It didn't matter how far I dragged the trough in the darkness, the mozzies always followed in hot pursuit. They were eager for a piece of me.

Frustrated beyond belief, I decided to have another crack at an underground chamber on top of the dam wall, using the trough as a roof. All I had to do was dig into the top of the dam bank to provide my four walls. It wouldn't look very pretty, but surely it would be more practical than lying on the ground.

I set to work to build my new fortress on top of the big green mound. By positioning it east to west, I could watch the sun rise and set from the relative comfort of inside.

Measuring the length and width of the trough with my walking stick, I carved an outline about 200 centimetres long and 90 centimetres wide into the dirt. After that, it was simply a matter of excavating into the hard earth.

I proceeded to spend the whole day either on the end of my stick or swinging a star picket I'd found attached to the trough. I was copping an unreal pounding from the sun, even early in the mornings, but the hole wasn't about to dig itself.

By the end of the second day of this, I'd managed a hole about 30 centimetres deep. It was just enough for me to turn over inside my humpy without being squashed against the ceiling.

Digging, sweating, digging. There seemed to be no end to how deep I could go if I put in the effort.

Despite the recent rain, the ground was tough to plough into. It almost buckled me. Desperate for some kind of relief from the relentless sun, I used my stick and the star picket to prop up one end of the cattle trough. At least that way I could keep digging in the shade it provided, using another star picket I'd found lying in the grass.

Having my stick and the star picket jacked up like that gave me the idea of packing mountains of reinforced mud under the trough's sides. Here I was sweating my arse off, digging under a hot tin roof, when I could be building the walls up to sit the trough on top of.

It was a method that would provide me with an effective insulator, and it was a whole lot easier on my weary muscles. I liked that idea. Collect mud for high walls, instead of busting my arse digging in the dirt.

The next few days consisted of much the same routine. In the morning I would get up and have a swim, and then do a food run. Then I'd get stuck into some more building. At the end of the day I'd scamper through the paddock to collect more food.

* * *

Towards the end of my first week at the dam, a plane flew directly over me. It was a few hundred feet in the air and I waved and screamed myself silly, as if it was within arm's reach.

I wasn't too concerned when the pilot didn't notice my ranting performance. I just assumed that, since I'd seen one hover so close already, it would only be a matter of time before one saw me eventually. I appeared to be under some kind of outback flight path and only needed one observant pilot to spot me or my camp.

Not long after making this observation, I came closer to being spotted from the air than at any other time during my desert incarceration. But unfortunately, that was also the last time I encountered an aircraft, near or far.

It started out as a little black dot hovering in the distance. I thought it was another plane on what I assumed was its regular mail run. As the little black dot moved closer, I figured out it wasn't a plane, but a helicopter. More than likely, being on such a remote cattle property, it was a muster chopper. Amazingly, it was flying just above the tree line—and heading straight for me.

I realised this was my best chance yet to achieve a rescue. Grabbing the biggest branches I could find, I jumped on top of my humpy. I disregarded the burning sensation in my feet. The prickles covering the bark pierced my hands, I was holding them so tightly, but I didn't mind that either.

Yelling, screaming, waving, I could almost touch the underside of his chopper. He flew so close on approach, I could read the letters identifying the aircraft. He couldn't have been flying any higher than 15 metres above the ground.

He appeared to be looking right between my eyes. I could even see the expression on his face. I could almost feel him touching the foot pedals. I was ecstatic and began looking around the paddock for the best place for him to land.

But he didn't. He flew directly over my one-man demo, without a second thought.

Christ knows what the idiot pilot was looking at. How he could've missed me screaming at him, I have no idea. He just cruised over the top of me jumping and yelling frantically and continued on his merry way.

My voice became hollow again. I dropped my branches in disgust, swearing and cursing. At the same time, I tried to remain optimistic. If I'd come so close to being saved after just a week at the dam, my days here had to be numbered.

How wrong can a person be? I would've thrown rocks at his rotor blades if I'd have known what was to come. He could have shared my misery for the next 40-odd days.

In hindsight, I should've realised that the last thing a pilot would be looking for out there was a desperate man on the brink of starvation. Flapping my hands like a sparrow in a stiff breeze wouldn't make any difference.

Even if he did see me, there was no guarantee he would stop. For all I knew, he'd probably just think I was a station hand working on the property, waving at him to say hello.

12

FOOD FOR THOUGHT

After dealing with the disappointment of being ignored, I settled back into my daily routine. Each day, my humpy got a little bit bigger and more comfortable. I carted load after load of mud in my converted shirt curtains and packed it on the inside.

There were heaps of mud to collect from the edge of the dam and I approached my new task like a one-man conveyor belt. Dig, carry and build. Up and down the bank all day, until it was time for a swim or a food run.

I repeated this pattern for days and weeks on end, constantly striving to make my home more comfortable. From end to end I worked. I'd build up one side and then move the star picket support to lift the other and resume the regime.

I knew I'd have to pull out the star picket I used as a support beam on the inside and start again. I found another star picket near the perimeter of the dam. The star pickets

The Boree intersection. Which way to go?

Ricky sitting on what was his final humpy on the edge of the big green mound.

Ricky's humpy in proximity to the dam that kept him alive in the last weeks.

Ricky taking a peek through the eastern side of his humpy.

Ricky pulling dirt out of his humpy at the first dam on his return to the station.

The tree stump next to the Boree intersection that hid the life-threatening centipede.

The rotten tooth Ricky pulled out with the help of his car keys.

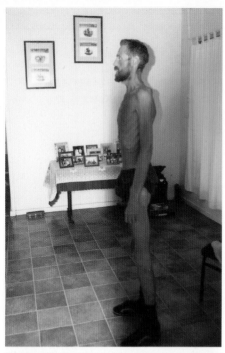

A profile of Ricky hours after he was found by station hands.

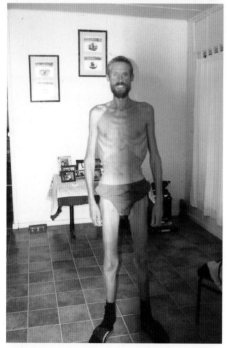

All smiles after a miraculous survival.

Ricky enjoying a strawberry milkshake and a hamburger after being released from hospital.

Ricky's final statement—a cross to mark what he thought would be his grave.

gave shape to the mountains of mud that I packed in around them before pulling them out for the next building phase. Lifting that bloody trough while I built two mud pillars for walls and then four—two on each end—was mind-numbing, but it gave me something to do.

Days and weeks of carting and digging. Layer upon layer of mud caked hard by the sun to form my four walls. Carting the mud wasn't easy when I could feel myself getting weaker by the hour. It amazed me how much I could pack inside those two halves of my t-shirt.

I didn't think about much else early in the construction phase. All my efforts went into building a fortress capable of prolonging my survival against the elements. Plus, thinking about my problems only frustrated me more. I was used to hard manual labour and felt happy to at least have something to do.

To an outsider, I would have looked like one of those storks with a newborn baby under my wing, carrying my mud bundles under each arm. If only there had been an outsider to notice me.

I packed so much mud in my t-shirt bundles sometimes that I wondered if I'd even be able to pick them up. They were so heavy, I'd be left swinging in the breeze for a couple of steps until my arms could take the strain and I regained my balance. Pour the mud into place and repeat the process. My whole day was devoted to building the sides up higher before the sun went down.

I just kept packing mud and bringing back bits of a petrol tank I'd found or anything else I could drag back from the busted water pump near the cattle yards a few hundred metres away. I was targeting anything that could be used as supports under the old trough to keep the process going while I balanced the star pickets to hold my humpy up.

So much mud went into that thing. I basically removed a whole section of the dam wall to make it liveable. It looked like an excavator had been to work on a construction site, yet I'd used only my bare hands to cart the load.

With so much mud packed inside for insulation, my shirt curtains also acted as a heat regulator. In the morning, I'd leave the curtains open to collect the breeze to cool the inside. As the afternoon wore on, I shut them to retain overnight the heat generated by my tin roof during the day.

I had only to think of the mozzies for motivation, whenever I stopped to wonder why I was putting in so much effort for such a small reward. I knew they'd be waiting for me if I didn't reach my building goal each day.

Sometimes I managed a few hours' peace, but I was always left wondering where the next bite would come from. I just kept having to make improvements to the humpy until they couldn't bzzz through its curtained ends anymore.

They only needed a little hole to appear through my curtains, or else they'd find the smallest crevice in the walls. Then it was goodnight to a good night's sleep. I couldn't imagine how bad they would be if I didn't have a half-decent shelter. I'd be left wanting to die.

Because of these challenges, I mostly just got on with the job without complaint. But there were days when I considered throwing in the towel and taking it easy.

The most notable of these occurred one windy afternoon when my chocked-up humpy came crashing down on me.

One strong gust and I was left staring at the sky's blue ceiling. The trough banged my head and almost knocked me unconscious.

Needless to say, it bloody hurt. But there was no point complaining; I was pretty sure nobody would hear my feeble screams of protest. And it made me a lot more wary of falling humpies in the future.

Finally, I had a humpy with 120 centimetres of head clearance on the inside and 90 centimetres wide. A midget could stand up and not bump his head.

I had learned early in the building trade that even the roughest of dwellings on the outside could double their value if they were clean and practical. With that in mind, it occurred to me that sleeping on dirt was a bit rugged. I wanted to do it in style and gathered mountains of grass to make a soft mattress.

Once that was done, I started to mould shelves inside the humpy so I could store my food stashes there. I used the worn-out knees of my shorts that I'd been wearing as a cap and made them into napkins to keep my bopples dry and clean.

As an alternative to the taste of burnt froggy flesh when I cooked on the trough roof, I hung the wire skewers from the star picket at the entrance of my humpy to dry them out. The breeze cooled the inside of my humpy if I opened the curtains through the day. It also slowly dried out any skewered frogs that were hanging from the wire attached to the star picket. It worked like a frog-jerky maker.

This method also eliminated the risk of my frogs being swooped on by birds or hobbling off the tin plate. I could watch them dry out in front of me from the cool comfort of my humpy.

My prized water tin had a spot reserved for it on the shelf I'd crafted from a star picket that also acted as a support beam at my humpy entrance. On this shelf I was also able to store larger stashes of bopples. That meant I had more to gorge on throughout the night.

In between my regular food runs, I always spent time improving or reinforcing my humpy. I concentrated on chipping away inside and out to relieve the boredom. Not until the last couple of weeks was I completely satisfied. There was always more mud to cart.

But no matter how painstakingly I built my mud walls, they couldn't stop the rain from penetrating in a good downpour. That familiar pitter-patter could be bittersweet. It meant the bopples would be big and juicy the next morning. But when a big storm did hit, I could forget about going to sleep. If it really pissed down, I'd have to spend the next few hours sweating on my hands and knees trying to shore up the foundations from the inside.

It would start with a splatter, then a ball of mud falling on my face, then my whole fucking house would start to fall in on top of me. Unless I madly slapped the dripping mud back against the walls to support the star pickets that acted as my foundations, I would be wearing a disaster. My walls would come crashing down around my ears and I'd be back out in the elements gathering more mud to make hasty home renovations in the darkness.

One big chunk all but concussed me one night after it hit me square on the forehead while I was enjoying a deep slumber. I didn't know what was going on. It felt like someone had thrown a rock at me from a great height.

From then on, even the slightest hint of a storm kept me awake for the whole night, just in case I didn't wake up at all. My fear of having to rebuild kept me constantly occupied, even when it wasn't raining.

That's where my stick came in handy. What it lacked in penetration, it more than made up for in reliability. Sometimes I found myself talking to it about stuff only we could relate to. Why has no one come searching for us? How much longer are we going to be stuck out here? If only it had had the capacity to talk back.

Nothing lasted forever out in the desert though, not even my stick. One night I woke up and half my humpy was washed away and I panicked.

Fair's fair, rain's rain, but that was a lot of mud to contend with and I was out of star pickets to support any frantic midnight renovations. They'd all been encased in the mud walls for reinforcement. The only way to stop my humpy from collapsing into a pile of mud was to pack in more and shore the sides up with something solid.

I crawled outside my humpy to pack the sides in the pelting rain, but there was so much water the mud just melted. I needed something to give structure to my desperate effort.

Suddenly I thought of my stick. If I packed some mud around it at the base, it might hold until the morning and I could finally get some fucking sleep.

So much mud, for so little sleep. Finally the rain eased and the mud held semi-solid around my stick. It was just sufficient to allow me to close my eyes without fear of the walls caving in on top of me.

The next morning, my stick didn't even cross my mind when I first woke up. I felt so tired I didn't even think about where it had ended up until late in the afternoon.

Shit, my walking stick! I suddenly realised it was still buried in the base of my humpy, but I was too tired to dig it out and I decided to search for its remains later. About four months later, as it turned out, after being saved from certain death and returning here to document my ordeal.

* * *

My adventure with the water monitor underlined my positive approach to getting out alive. If not well fed, then at least my survival instincts were well honed.

I'd hatched a good plan to snatch the sneaky water monitor that had been lurking around the dam for some time. It was a plan I'd thought long and hard about after several days of observation.

My humpy was well sorted back then. I'd gained some extra energy with a regular diet of frogs and vegetation and thought the time was ripe for a carnivorous feast.

It was my dam after all. Any creature that wanted to stake a claim was welcome to apply. I was happy to personally stamp their passport with my teeth and throw their measly bones to the ants.

The idea was to pounce on the cunning bastard when he wasn't looking. I'd have him hog-tied and cooking on the heat of my humpy before sundown—I licked my lips in anticipation, just thinking about the prospect.

But my plan's execution was as comical as it was painful. I was sitting on the side of the dam, acting inconspicuous as always, when the water monitor strolled over the top of the grassy mound. He was pretty cluey, even though he moved around in full view like he owned the place. I knew I'd probably only get one good crack at him.

He kept a good eye on me as he swam laps around the dam's perimeter, while I watched him like a hawk. When he lost sight of me for a moment, I decided to put my plan into action. I ran over to the opposite bank, where he was headed, and waited patiently.

Sitting in the long grass, I could see him perched on the water's edge, looking hurriedly around for me. To try and hide from his prying eyes, I camouflaged myself with grass and crawled a bit closer. It was all going to plan until we locked eyes and he quickly swam away effortlessly.

We replayed this charade for about the next half an hour. Neither of us wanted to concede an inch to the other.

Finally, I thought I'd outmanoeuvred him when I hid behind a clump of thorny bushes right next to where he emerged from the water. Not even he thought I would be stupid enough to ambush him through so much skin-scraping foliage.

I knew it was going to hurt, pouncing through the thorns like that to grab hold of him. But I reasoned the pain would be well worth the satisfaction of sucking on his juicy burnt flesh.

He took a few tentative steps out of the water. He still appeared wary of my presence, but confident enough to expose himself. I geed myself up as he nudged closer, ready to accept the blood and the scratches I was bound to cop for the sake of a good feed.

With nothing to lose but my own blood, I ploughed through the bushes in a swathe of swearing and cursing from the impact of the thorns. They hurt just as much as I had anticipated.

Despite landing face-first in the dirt, I somehow managed to grab hold of his thrashing tail. He stood there stunned by the absurdity of my surprise attack, but it didn't take him long to react. He quickly regained his composure and whipped his tail through my hands like the slip of a tongue. In a flash, he was back into the safety of the water.

I was left writhing in pain, nursing the chunks missing from my sunburnt head. In defeat, the blood dripped from my skinned chest and scratched elbows.

I'd basically headbutted the ground while diving for him. Plunging down the dam bank forehead first, with my nose and face scraping the dust as I lunged forward, probably hadn't been such a good idea after all. My eyes were seeing stars for a few moments, but I tried to pull myself together to restore some sense of dignity to my hunting efforts.

When I finally refocused, I locked onto the arrogant little bastard swimming across the dam as if nothing had happened. I picked myself up out of the dust and dived into the dam in hot pursuit. My pride hurt much more than my bleeding wounds.

I fixed my gaze on him gliding through the clear water. He swam effortlessly towards the opposite bank. Was he giving me another chance, or simply taunting me?

Whatever his reasons, I decided to have another crack for the sake of a feed of substance. By his reaction, I don't think he planned to let me get so close the second time around either.

It certainly spooked him. I probably would've had him clutched in my hands if I'd dived under the water and grabbed him from below. Instead, I tried to sneak up on him quietly on the surface, pretending to be invisible.

One glimpse of my ugly head staring back at him and— bang!—he was off. He clambered out of the dam in a shot and pegged it up to the safety of the bank.

Meanwhile, I was left feeling stupid and sore from my useless attempts. Cursing myself, I swam back to my humpy to lick my wounds. There was skin off my nose and my hand hurt from where he had whipped me. I had to pay him his dues for giving me such a thorough flogging.

When the water monitor came back to the dam for a swim a few days later, he made sure to keep both eyes on me. But now I was only looking on as a curious observer. I still enjoyed watching him swimming around, peering at me so defensively. He didn't let me out of his sight for a second, just in case I had other ideas about sticking him onto my makeshift frypan.

At this time, I thought it didn't matter so much and there would be other decent-sized animals to eat. I just had to be patient. Maybe I just needed to stick to frogs and leeches that didn't fight back.

But then another diversion from the daily boredom at the dam arrived in the shape of a family of ducks that moved into my patch. Ducks are very cute, I know, but they can also be cunning little fuckers. Even more so than water monitors.

Mama and Papa Duck just swanned into the dam out of the blue one day. They had four or five little baby duckies in tow who obviously had yet to learn how to fly, judging by their fruitless flapping. They provided me with much amusement, attempting to take off with their baby wings, trying to figure out how they worked. Watching them counteracted the monotony of my life that consisted of simply existing and not much else.

As soon as I saw them, my first gung-ho thoughts were to just jump in. I'd have me a couple of little duckies for dinner, no worries. But then I figured it would be more satisfying to watch them fatten up for a more complete feast.

After they made a few more visits though, my stomach began to rumble for something to eat besides frogs and bopples. I thought I could grab at least one of the little babies as a rewarding snack—surely they wouldn't notice one missing? I could leave the rest of the family for a more substantial meal later.

I reckon the parents had me pegged as a predator straightaway on the afternoon I decided to dive on in for my fill of fried duck meat. It was like they smelt my carnivorous intentions as soon as they slipped into the water.

The little duckies swam in formation behind big Mama, with Papa Duck bringing up the rear. I crept around the other side of the dam and hid in the metre-long grass, waiting for my opportunity to pluck one of the babies when they wandered past.

Mama Duck waddled off into the long grass right near me, with her little ducklings in hot pursuit. At the same time, Papa Duck began staggering about in the shallows like he'd just suffered a terminal injury.

I figured there was no point chasing after the little ones with Papa Duck in such distress. Disregarding where the rest of the posse had escaped to, I set my sights on the patriarch of the family.

He looked half-dead sitting there on the water's edge. I walked up confidently, for what I assumed would be an easy kill with my bare hands. But, just as I was about to whack him into next week, he came back stronger than Lazarus.

His resurrection was too quick for me and he flew off without a care in the world. The dirty little bastard was foxing me all along to enable his family to escape undetected.

I was freaking out that I'd missed another opportunity to chew on meat that real people eat. I then began searching frantically for the path the rest of the duck family had followed, driven by spite more than anything. I wanted to eat the whole family for dinner for showing me up in my own backyard. My revenge would be swift and merciless.

But it was like scrambling to find a particular grain of sand at the beach. My efforts to search for their little footsteps in such a huge area were futile. I came up with nothing more than a few grass stains and a badly beaten ego.

I think the duck family moved to another suburb of the desert after their close call with Ricky Megee. Certainly they never returned to my dam.

* * *

I put particular effort into trying to light a fire. Sitting there in the dismal darkness on the bank of the dam, I hoped and wondered about how to do it. If I could get a fire going, my chances of living through this nightmare would grow with each flickering flame.

Not only would a fire provide warmth, but I could cook with it. Staring at the flames dancing in the moonlight would also be a welcome distraction from the blackness of the night.

There weren't many methods I didn't experiment with. Rubbing sticks together, flicking rocks to create a spark, using the sun to ignite a bushfire or praying to God for a nearby lightning strike.

Lightning—it could've been my greatest salvation but in the end it was one more frustration. If one of the nearby trees took a direct hit from a fierce bolt and smouldered for a moment, I thought I could throw handfuls of dry grass on it. That would give me enough kindling to build the flames up with branches to defeat any downpour.

Watching the electric skies of a lightning storm with nothing but hope, I followed every bolt to the ground. But it was futile. It appeared even the lightning had it in for me. All I got out of it was a good soaking while waiting and watching for my chance.

The obvious method was to rub sticks together. It worked for the blackfellas and I'd seen it happen in the movies. How hard could it be?

I rubbed those sticks together so hard and fast I almost developed callouses on my hands. Generating electricity from the energy created by my furious rubbing would've been an easier feat.

Rocks. There were plenty of rocks around. I crashed them together with such force that the echo spread across the paddock for miles. Sure enough, I managed momentary sparks in the process. But getting those sparks to spread to flames proved impossible.

Returning to my humpy, I picked up a star picket and jabbed it against the metal posts that acted as the support beams of my humble dwelling. Once again, I could generate a spark easy enough. I even had bunches of dry grass strategically placed to capture the brightest flickers. But I was left with nothing but sore arms.

Jabbing my star picket at the metal roof of my humpy returned the same result—nil. The arseholes who scavenged the lighter from my pocket before leaving me for dead had done me over yet again.

* * *

My mind wandered constantly. The frustration of seeing those idiot pilots behind the controls who didn't look down in those first crucial days at the dam gnawed at me.

Simply existing had become my new strategy. I'd become disillusioned about my prospects of being rescued and had run out of ideas to make someone notice me. Some days I'd spend the entire afternoon just sitting under a tree, waiting for a plane or a chopper to fly past, just in case.

The whole time out there, I was thinking about it. I wasn't a bad person; there was no reason why I should have ended up dead in the middle of bloody nowhere like that.

You wouldn't leave a dog to die out there, like that mob had done to me.

This feeling of desertion played on my mind. I felt at a complete loss as to why such a bastard act should be played out on me. How could someone do that to another human being, and walk away? One minute I was driving to Port Hedland; the next I was in a hole in the fucking desert.

My feelings of revenge had mostly subsided by that stage. No bad deed I'd ever done could compare to such horror. Nothing short of putting those responsible for my predicament through the same torment would compensate. But doing that would get me nowhere and thinking about it only deepened my misery.

* * *

My energy levels were being depleted and so were my food sources. When I first arrived I could catch six to eight big frogs a day without too much trouble. But by about my third week at the dam, I could only manage two or three smaller ones. And it took a lot more time and effort for this petty harvest.

I thought I must have eaten all the parents and was quickly gobbling up all the baby froggies. In the hope of getting their numbers up, I gave the frogs a rest for a while. I stuck to grasshoppers and my bush tucker vegetarian diet.

Unfortunately, the leeches also appeared to have left the building. My ravenous appetite for dining on those delicacies again appeared to have all but eliminated them from the menu as well.

A fair proportion of my survival could be explained by my own mindset. If I complained about anything, I'd get stuff-all the next day, when suddenly the frogs and leeches wouldn't want to know about me and the bopple bushes would seem further from each other than before. But if I praised God for giving me nothing, then all the luck seemed to come my way the next morning. It was that much easier to catch the slippery frogs and the leeches that stuck to my tongue tasted more nourishing. All of a sudden, my pockets weren't big enough to hold all the bopples I could collect in just a short spurt, whereas the day before I'd had to walk for miles for a paltry meal.

About the only thing to cheer me up out there was a visit from the one friend I made in the desert. Unfortunately, he wasn't human and had no prospects of getting me out of there alive. But the companionship of a one-eyed dingo can never be underestimated.

He was like a pet dog, except he was wild. I also couldn't feed him much because I was slowly starving to death myself.

I was a bit sceptical when he first arrived on the scene, as he was very flighty around me. But then I had a closer look at him and understood why. His right eye showed obvious signs he'd been on the losing end of a fair old fight which had claimed his sight.

But not even the friendship of old Bung-Eye would be enough to fend off reality. Food was what I needed most, and it was drying up as rapidly as my dams were becoming depleted from the lack of rain.

Finally, the day arrived when it didn't matter how devious I was—there were no more frogs to sneak up on and the leeches had either all gone too or worked out how to swim around me.

Originally, there had been insects to snack on everywhere and I had had plenty of wildlife. But as the weeks wore on and the paddock dried up, so did they.

No more frogs and no more leeches, but I could always rely on my bopples. My dependence on bopples as a reliable food source grew with each passing day. Even when they shrivelled to dangerously low levels, there were still enough around to keep me chewing if I put in the effort to collect them.

I would divide them up into piles after each successful food run. I'd put the ones with caterpillar holes in them in the 'to eat before the ants get into them' section and put the rest away on the shelf inside my humpy for later.

The big caterpillars that lived in the bopples went down as a much-needed sweet treat. I wasn't expecting to find caterpillars out there in the desert, especially not burrowing their weaselly holes inside my bopples before I picked them off the branch. The first one came as a bit of a shock. He was a little green fella about 2 centimetres long, but he tasted good. I wasn't about to start complaining. They weren't overly flavoursome—very squishy and gooey in texture. But they complemented the blandness of the bopples and ended up a satisfying find.

In reality, every caterpillar I swallowed actually doubled the food in my stomach. It meant they couldn't eat the few remaining bopples. I could get three or four chunky caterpillars out of just one bopple if I was lucky. The more of those I ate, the more bopples I could collect.

Ants loved bopples as much as the caterpillars and I did, so it became a pretty fierce competition. The holes carved into my bopples by the caterpillars created an entry point for an invasion by the ants that sat around waiting on my food shelf.

A couple of mornings, I woke up just to discover empty husks that had been delicious bopples the night before. I realised I had to sort out this problem fast or I would end up sharing my stash with the ants. So I adopted the rule that only the caterpillarless bopples would be kept on my shelf each night. The rest went straight to my stomach.

Some people like to eat big slabs of meat; others enjoy lentil soup. Ants don't care what they eat. They even chewed on me when there was nothing else to munch on.

I tried eating them for revenge, but they were more of a nuisance than a meal. Besides, there were too many of them to put a dent in the population.

It became a matter of survival. I was determined to eat better than the caterpillars and the ants combined. My determination was all I had left to battle my growing weakness.

I even ate a wasp once. That was a fair indication of the pathetic levels I'd stoop to for a feed. As soon as I saw him, I knew I had to at least have a go. I would have swallowed anything by then.

I was just sitting there in my humpy, slowly starving, when he flashed by. An intriguing and potentially succulent new food source buzzing about my head. Of all the places in the world where that stupid wasp could have been, he had to come and check out mine in the middle of nowhere. I thought he deserved to be eaten on the grounds of stupidity alone. With not much other ammunition available, I grabbed for my shorts lying next to me. I didn't hesitate as I wound up for a hefty swing at him; I wanted to see how succulent he tasted.

That first crack stunned him enough to drop to the ground. I eagerly picked up his shattered remains out of the grass of my mattress and delicately plucked out his stingers, before sending him down the food chute.

Unfortunately, it was a sadly disappointing experience for both of us. A waste of my time and his existence. Instead of the sweet honey flavour I had been hoping for, I was dished up a lacklustre shell of nothingness. It could only be compared to munching on a crunchy piece of fresh air. Bloody ordinary by anyone's standards, and not worth the time and effort it took to bring him down.

There was no point me holding a grudge, though. I was literally fading away to nothing. I quietly cursed myself and snapped back into reality.

Food, water, shelter. These were my basic requirements to survive and I seemed to have them all covered to start with. Yet as the days wore on and I wore out, I had to look around for eating alternatives that didn't require expending so much valuable energy.

But even I had a breaking point. My next new victim will be remembered as without a doubt the most disgusting pile of shit that ever passed my lips. It almost tipped me over the edge of resilience.

Over the previous few weeks, I'd observed the odd cockroach invade my humpy. They mostly landed at night as I was trying to catch some sleep. I decided that on the off chance they actually tasted half decent, it was worth the risk to try and digest one.

What if, for whatever gross reason, they were edible? I wouldn't have to waste so much energy walking for miles to collect food. There were enough cockroaches sneaking around to fill my snack quota for weeks. How bad could they really be?

The ones crawling through my space were big buggers, that was for sure. Measuring a good few centimetres long and half as thick, they seemed to be moving into the neighbourhood without any invitation. It didn't seem to matter whether I liked how they tasted or not.

Determined to go through with my sickening experiment, I stuck my hand out and grabbed one of the filthy bastards. With my hands firmly clasped around him, I hesitated over whether to eat the head or the bum first. I wasn't sure where to begin with such a vile creature.

Deciding in the end that it didn't really matter, I brought him close to my face to look him square in the eyes. Then I cancelled his passport to life.

Just bringing that putrid, disgusting thing near my mouth created a smell strong enough to make me want to spew. But there was still the remote possibility they tasted like peaches—I had to go through with it.

My resistance to toxic tastes was pretty high by that stage. I ignored the stench and shoved him head-first into my hungry mouth.

I'm not sure if it was the stomach-churning taste or the smell that got me in the end. However, the result was putrid enough to have me hurling uncontrollably out the end of my humpy within two seconds. I didn't even manage to chew on him in the end—he was spat out before he sucked his last breath.

That taste was enough to contaminate my mouth with his filth for at least a few days. Even seeing one of those awful creatures crawling around after that made me feel a bit sick in the guts. They are without a doubt the epitome of all things disgusting.

13

GOODBYE BUNG-EYE

Food was becoming scarcer by the mouthful. Even a lot of the vegetation had stretched out of my reach. I'd become that hard up for something to eat, I resorted to swatting march flies for nourishment.

They didn't taste too bad actually, for flies. They were big enough to have a bite out of, anyway. I counted them as another win for the hungry skinny people.

I knew I'd eaten a fly, that's for sure. But they tasted pretty sweet in the circumstances. They had a raw and meaty substance to them, like a rare steak when you like it well done.

Regardless of their size, the flies were generally pretty quick off the mark. I had to let them bite me first and get settled on my skin before I squashed them. Once I saw their little stingers protruding, it was a matter of bingo and there you go. They were scooped up and deposited into my mouth in the blink of an eye.

I spotted one of those big fluffy black caterpillars sitting around the humpy one afternoon and thought I might as well give him a go as well. I wasn't too sure whether to eat him or not at first. All I could remember was being told as a kid not to touch them because they're dangerous.

I threw him into my water tin to drown while I considered my options. Childhood advice wasn't enough to save him. He was going down the hatch just like everything else.

He tasted a bit furry, which I suppose was to be expected. Swirling him around in my mouth, it felt a bit funny but seemed worth the discomfort. I squished him between my teeth and his flavour-filled guts splashed my gums. I couldn't detect any poison and felt glad to put that childhood myth to bed.

I learned early in the piece that, if something tasted a bit wrong or strange, I just had to shove in a few bopples or something else my body was used to. Generally, anything and everything went down the food chute.

I left it alone if the first mouthful really didn't taste right. With a supply of fresh water handy, I could wash my mouth out and hope that whatever I'd eaten didn't drop me. Put a dog turd in front of me and I probably would have swallowed it—I wasn't going to die not knowing.

Nothing with a hard crusty shell tasted any good, except for praying mantises. I tried to shy away from them because they've fascinated me since I was a little boy growing up on the farm, but they ended up as dinner four or five times. They had a surprisingly meaty texture for an insect. It was quite a delicacy, no matter how much it didn't feel right to be chowing down on them.

Despite their succulent flavour, it was hard to pinch one from his family, because of my childhood memories. But, on the flip side, I didn't want to create the kind of hunger problem I had when I let the blue-tongue lizard go by. They had to be swallowed for the sake of my empty stomach. There was no point dwelling on it.

If I ever found myself in a similar situation again, they'd be up the top of my menu for being such a tasty snack. And down the bottom for being the least deserving. But that didn't count for much out there.

One potential meal I didn't expect at my doorstep was a group of thirsty emus. I thought my big dream of carving up some serious wildlife was about to become a reality.

Four or five little ones, about a metre tall, wandered down to the dam one afternoon for a drink. I felt confident a couple of swings of the star picket would do the job on them, but those immature emus obviously had other ideas. As soon as I so much as looked at them twice, they were off.

I must have chased those little bastards through the paddock for close to a kilometre. I was running as fast as my sparrow-thin legs could carry me, waving my star picket above my head.

But just like the ducks and the planes and the cows before them, those thirsty emus never came back. I had to give up on yet another impossible meal.

Another close encounter with a real feed was when I walked straight past a smallish kangaroo. I was out collecting bopples in the paddock one afternoon and almost trod on him.

I was just walking along, minding my own business as usual, when all of a sudden this little kangaroo bounced up out of the grass. He was no more than a couple of metres away when he noticed me in his sleep and took off in fright.

He looked just as startled to see me as I was to spot him and he wasted no time jumping to his spring-injected feet. Before I could even be bothered putting in the big steps to chase him down, he'd bounded away.

I thought about running after him for a moment. But I didn't like my chances of catching a frightened kangaroo at the best of times, let alone when I was on the brink of starvation.

He scared the crap out of me, to be honest. It came as such a surprise to see another living creature in such close proximity. By the look on his startled face, he was just as alarmed to see me patrolling the paddock. He just got off the mark quicker.

I caught sight of another kangaroo in similar circumstances not long afterwards. But once again, I wasn't thinking about collaring wildlife at the time and he bolted before I could blink.

* * *

The bigger animals I wasn't any good at catching. This caused me no end of frustration. No—the cows, the baby emus and kangaroos simply ran too fast for me. Instead, I had an abundance of putrid cockroaches.

But why hadn't someone found me yet? It had been more than a month since the mob dumped me, and nothing.

Thanks for the food and the rain and everything, God, but why aren't I dead? What's going on with the big picture here? What am I here for if I'm still alive, and how much longer do I have to take this shit for?

My bones were poking out of my skin and my eyes were sinking into my head. Never in my worst nightmares could I have imagined getting so thin. I wasn't sure how anorexic people felt before they died, but I figured I must have been pretty bloody close.

Maybe there are a couple of weeks left in me—three, if I'm really lucky. On the flip side, I could die tomorrow. I dunno.

I had been a little worried about my weight at the first dam, but I never dwelt on it too much. What was the point? But a month or so into life at my second waterhole and the seriousness of my situation had sunk in.

It was unreal how fast the weight could drop off me. I could sit in my humpy and watch the muscle literally wasting off my bones. I'd eaten crabs, leeches, frogs and bugs—you name it and I'd at least tried to digest it. Yet I still couldn't accomplish a bulging belly. What did I have to do to pack on a few pounds? Eat myself maybe?

My ribs were sticking out; as I lay on my grass mattress they poked deeper into the floor by the hour. Bones that I didn't previously know existed jabbed into me.

I couldn't cup my hands together to get a drink without the water seeping through the gap between them. My arse cheeks didn't even touch anymore. It was unreal. My eyelids didn't shut tight either when I closed them, or put my head under water, no matter how tight I squeezed.

I'd lost so much weight, my calf and thigh muscles had virtually disappeared. Half my skeleton was protruding. It surprised me someone could get so skinny and not be completely dysfunctional. I thought all those organs getting squashed up on my insides would have caused some pretty severe damage internally.

I decided things couldn't be that bad; I was a pretty big fella before they dumped me. But there seemed to be only a few kilos separating me and starvation. Short of digesting a cow, there didn't seem to be a lot around to fatten up my reserves.

Trying to put weight back on with such a paltry diet was like eating soup with a fork. Even shoving my face with bopples twice a day and chewing on frogs and leeches couldn't stop me from daily losing a kilo plus.

Get food so you don't die, Rick! That's all I had to keep telling myself.

I didn't mind sweating myself into the dust if I returned from a food run with my pockets full of bopples. As long as I had a few left over to nibble on in the morning, I felt pretty satisfied.

But if I had a lean afternoon, there'd be plenty of swearing and cursing on the long walk back to my empty humpy. The more the hunger pains grumbled, the more I knew I had to get something to eat or I was fucked.

It finally came time to chop my food runs in half. The vegetation was running out and I knew it was going to be a struggle I couldn't win.

I separated the paddock into four parts to allow the vegetation more time to grow. By methodically harvesting one section per daily food run, I hoped to extend my survival.

I chose the late afternoon rather than the early mornings to stuff my pockets with food. It was cooler and gave me something to look forward to at the end of each day.

The area immediately surrounding the dam had been full of bopple bushes when I first arrived. But over the weeks, I'd slowly eaten myself out of house and home. I lacked the stamina to reach the far corners of the paddock.

It wasn't raining much, so the majority of my food sources had dried up. Even my once pristine dam had turned murky from the dead grass rising to the surface.

Realistically, for how long could I go on? With only half the calories, I wasn't sure. My motivation dropped off me as my energy levels took a hammering. I hardly recognised my reflection in the dam.

Me and Bung-Eye were more or less competing for the same food, which was pretty scarce. He shadowed me for a few days, hanging around my humpy until I ventured out for a food run. I wasn't sure if he was waiting for me to die so he could have a piece of my skinny arse.

He always trailed behind me a few feet while I scrambled through the paddock searching for bopples. He'd rush up and wait patiently when I sat down to harvest the spindly bushes.

Sleeping had become the best part of the day for me. It was the only escape from the fractured torment of reality. If for some reason I couldn't go out on my afternoon food run, my physical deterioration kicked me down. I'd taken a step closer to starvation by not going anywhere. It didn't matter if it poured down rain and reinvigorated the vegetation enough to sustain me for two daily food runs, I was convinced my legs wouldn't carry me to the next bopple bush.

I couldn't help but notice the depth of the water in my dam dwindling. Now I could easily stand in parts where before I hadn't been able to touch the bottom, and my feet were becoming tangled in the weeds. The overflow dams on either side had dried rock-hard.

The dam was also a good indicator of my overall health. It supported most of my routine each day, whether it be collecting mud for my humpy, splashing around for a drink or searching for food. So when it went to shit, then so did I.

I was always thinking about the nourishing taste of meat, from what I could remember of it. Anything of significance would have been appreciated. Even the smallest of animals would have made a splendid meal.

Old Bung-Eye was still hanging around. He looked a bit scrawny himself, but he wasn't as starving as me. He reminded me of a one-eyed mate I had back in Brisbane, who had lost his sight in the same eye after someone hit him with a dart. I coaxed the dingo towards me with a few bopples and he gladly complied.

It became clear that he wasn't hanging around just to eat my corpse. Out of boredom, I talked to him. He provided a welcome distraction to the depressing reality of my meagre existence.

I'd chat to Bung-Eye about simple things like what we had to do that day for each of us to stay alive. He didn't appear too interested in my planned routine but was content to let me verbalise it, to imagine we were having a normal conversation. I just felt glad to go over things in my head with another living creature.

He kept coming back, and I wondered if I should stake him with my star picket. I weighed it up, but these were only the fleeting thoughts of a desperate man. It would have been impossible to throw him on the humpy for dinner when he reminded me so much of my mate back home. That bung-eyed dingo was the closest thing I had to a mate out there. I felt this strange attachment to him.

Then one morning, Bung-Eye just didn't turn up. I assumed he must have just wandered off.

I didn't worry about it too much as I had my own problems to deal with. Maybe he had just got sick of waiting for me to give up.

Nutriment from the vegetation had kept me alive, but I craved the protein of a big juicy steak. Instead, I simply became thinner and weaker. I was more desperate, and less certain I could survive.

The oblivious muster choppers and mail planes that had flown straight over me were all but forgotten. Why had I bothered waving my hands when the stupid pilots only kept their eyes on the sky dead ahead?

I didn't even think about getting saved anymore—there seemed to be no point. Thinking about it just made me depressed. I retained the will to survive, but all hope of rescue appeared lost.

What if I couldn't be bothered one day and died quietly? Would anyone ever know I had been there? Making my humpy mozzie- and rain-proof was all I had to do to keep me going. It was hardly a reason to live, but entirely necessary.

The ants working themselves into a frenzy inside my humpy were a good sign that a storm was rolling in. I knew that meant more midnight mud-carting was ahead. But at least a good downpour would transform the landscape into a lush green sea.

Then rain finally poured down. I sat up, all prepared to launch into salvage mode, but not one drop penetrated my little mudbrick fortress. No rain penetration and basically mozzie-proof. It had taken more than a month of fine-tuning, but I'd finally managed to construct the humpy I set out to make all those hundreds of hours ago.

My sense of accomplishment was heightened by my knowledge that all I had had, in order to achieve such an outstanding outcome, was what nature had provided me. I had nothing else except for a bit of tin, a few star pickets, my stick, a hardened instinct and the will to survive.

I did make one final attempt to walk out of there. But it didn't take too many steps to realise that hiking was about my worst option.

Still, I gave it a try. I managed to get about 600 metres from the dam before collapsing to the ground completely sapped of energy. There was no way I was going any further. I had no hope of making it more than a kilometre.

I looked back and saw my humpy not that far away, but I was no longer capable of dragging my body off the ground. All I could do was lie there helplessly, with the sun pelting down on top of me.

Why turn around and go back, anyway? Why not just sit out in the sun and save my legs from having to make the same journey the next day to collect food. Maybe I could just stay out there and feast on the bopples for the night.

Mozzies changed that. They reminded me quick smart of the reasons why I lived in such an imposing shelter in the first place.

I slowly inched my way back towards a fresh mouthful of water, crawling miserably on my hands and knees all afternoon. The end of my pathetic effort to stagger back to the dam without dropping permanently coincided with the sunset skimming the water's surface. In another situation it would have looked sublime, but I no longer cared for pretty colours.

I forgot I no longer had the buoyancy to float and fell hopelessly into the dam, totally exhausted. Immersed in water too deep to stand up in, I somehow scrambled into the shallows, propelled by my feeble kicking and desperate dog-paddling.

I'd lived through so much horror, only to nearly drown through my own stupidity. One trivial episode with an almost fatal result. I vowed never to attempt another futile escape from my makeshift home on my own two feet.

Meanwhile, the bopples I'd been carrying were now bobbing in the water everywhere. Pockets full of them had gone to waste. To make things worse, I then discovered I had a humpy full of mozzies making themselves at home because I hadn't got back in time to close the curtains.

I was next to a dam that no one besides me seemed to remember or care about. How good was I going?

* * *

I didn't have to wait too long to figure out why old Bung-Eye had decided to make tracks and not come back. Maybe he saw the writing on the wall for both of us.

A few mornings later, instead of climbing out of my humpy to be greeted by my one-eyed mate, I woke up and was confronted by four dingoes. They seemed a lot less friendly than old Bung-Eye, and a lot more interested in the fact I was steadily starving to death.

Bung-Eye's mates made their intentions known pretty fast. They skirted around me menacingly and appeared to be as desperate for food as I was. Only they seemed intent on having a family feast.

Fucking dingoes. They're your best friend one minute and your own personal coffin carriers the next. But I had no intention of being another Azaria Chamberlain, neatly folded inside their clamped jaws.

From that moment on, making my humpy dingo-proof became my top priority. The gap created by my shirt curtain left plenty of room for a dingo to drag a carcass through. Since I was rapidly becoming a walking skeleton, I concentrated on closing up that hole as quickly as possible. I packed up each end of my humpy with armfuls of mud, so I could only squeeze in or out with a fair amount of effort. I didn't want to just disappear off the face of the earth without a trace and have no one know what happened to me. So when it looked like there was a chance the next night would be my last, I took steps to make sure they could pull my body from the humpy that was looking more and more like being my grave rather than my shelter. Every evening it became a routine to pack the entrance with some well-placed rocks in the hope that it would keep the dingoes at bay, long enough for someone to come along and find my remains if I died. Every night I did this it made me think more and more about the things I would miss and would never see or do again, like my family and friends. This became in itself extremely depressing; it was at this time I started to realise that I was losing faith and hope of ever being found. I found myself moping around a lot more and even finding it hard to motivate myself to find food and water. In actual fact, I think I had just come to the point that I was nearly ready to give up; I was nearly ready to die. As sad as it seems I think I was just hoping that it would hurry up and happen so that I could stop feeling like this.

I didn't want my remains scattered through the desert by dingoes and began making plans to orchestrate my own funeral. If I was going to die out there and have dingoes chew my dead flesh, it would be on my terms.

I wanted something left behind that my mum could bury when my remains were finally discovered. I made sure the scavengers would have to come inside and fight for their dinner. They might walk home with a full stomach, but at least they'd be empty-handed.

Imagining the poor person who would discover my body cheered me up, in a morbid kind of way. Someone was bound to find my abandoned car or report me missing eventually. Station hands would surely discover my corpse when they came to check on the dams.

Surely they would make the connection that I'd tried as best as I could to survive over a bloody long time and distance. My file wouldn't be stamped 'missing person' forever. They'd be kicking themselves for not finding me earlier.

With the pack of dingoes camped on my doorstep, I didn't have much else to do but keep a lonely vigil inside my humpy. When I wasn't asleep, I thought of the people I hadn't seen much of lately, but wished I'd spent more time with. I started to realise that there was a more than likely chance that I actually was going to die out here in the middle of nowhere, after throwing every ounce of strength and energy, both mental and physical, into staying alive. It finally hit me like a wrecking ball in the face that I would never see my family or friends again; that I had no children of my own that would carry on my name, which was something I never realised was important to me before; that there was no special person in my life that I loved and was loved by who would actually miss me if I died, apart from my mother. Not to mention things and places I had never done or seen. Thinking of all this at the time made me break down and cry. I couldn't believe this was it, that this was the end. It didn't feel right. *I can't go out like this, not like this.*

As a lover of food and a keen cook, I also dreamed of the dishes I wanted to create, if I ever made it out alive. There were so many different recipes I wanted to experiment with, I could let my imagination run wild.

I'm not sure if the dingoes grew bored of my reclusiveness, or just thought they'd come back later to collect their booty. After a few days of me being cooped up inside my solitary tomb, they made tracks and I was left on my own again. Hopefully old Bung-Eye escaped their wrath, as well.

The only times I emerged from my humpy after that was to have a swim in the morning or complete my solitary food run late in the afternoon. It was pretty easy to get depressed about the situation, but feeling sad didn't do my chances of survival any good.

On the bright side, it had been more than two months since I last had a cigarette. I'd probably kicked the habit.

I never really dwelt on all the good stuff I couldn't have out there, like alcohol or cigarettes. They were consigned to the ancient history of a civilisation that seemed well beyond my reach. There were more important factors for me to come to terms with—the heat, the mozzies, hunger, dehydration, the fact I'd been left for dead in the desert. The reality that no one seemed to know where I was, or give a fuck either way. I wasn't short on things to ponder.

Just when I thought things couldn't get any worse—short of dying, of course—they did. I woke up one morning with the whole left side of my mouth inexplicably swollen.

I initially suspected that a spider had bitten me during the night, the pain was so intense. To be honest, the consequences of that possibility didn't really bother me too much. *A spider's bitten me on the head? Great—kill me then, spider, I dare you!*

But I didn't die. To lessen the agony, I filled my head with random thoughts of a less violent nature. In my warped state of mind, I wondered what would happen if a cow walked up to the dam for a drink. I still had my vine with me—I felt pretty sure I could find the strength to lasso and eat one if I had the chance.

It also crossed my mind that if a cow did wander into my path, I could try and ride her to the next town. Although they don't move very fast, cows can walk for miles and generally know where they're going. They have to eat and drink as well.

I figured that, if I saddled one up, I could always keep my options open. Even if we ended up walking further into the desert, I could ultimately string my ride up, as though it were a takeaway meal on legs.

But it never came to that, because the cows ignored me. Instead, I was left to chew on the vegetation, just like a big dumb cow myself. I don't know how cows get so fat eating just grass.

The only escape from the mental and physical torture seemed to be to reflect on the absurdity of what a sorry joke my life had become. Crap pop songs from the 80s played through my head constantly. Random songs like 'What If God Was One Of Us'—the same bad tunes over and over.

Movies were another distraction. The scene from *Pulp Fiction* towards the end, when Samuel L. Jackson had his moment of clarity and the other guy was killed sitting on the dunny, summed up my situation. It played on my mind regularly—I just couldn't figure out which one I was meant to be.

And then there were the *Simpsons* episodes—all the things Homer had got away with over the years. Even when he ate too many chilli dogs and got lost in the desert after losing his marbles, he always found his way back to civilisation for thirds.

I chuckled regularly over that one. I knew I couldn't live my life as though it were a cartoon, but Homer gave me hope. If he could be so useless and get out of it, then so could I. It was like he was stuck out there with me.

I also used the time out there to invent new businesses and create new concepts. Things I never had the patience to explore before, in the rush of everyday living, I had no excuse not to pursue now. Homes for homeless kids; providing finance for Aussie battlers—I wanted to stop thinking about

myself so much and help other people less fortunate than me
if I could scrape through this nightmare.

I wished I had a pen and some paper to write down all
those random thoughts. But I had nothing to play with,
except the loose change still jangling in my pocket.

For whatever reason, I still had that $12.30 in my shorts.
Over the weeks and months I spent out there, I religiously
shined those coins with mud and polished them with my
shirt curtains, just in case I had to use them one day.

I wondered what my odds were to get a ticket through to
the pearly gates. That's where my dad and my grandparents
were, and I could do with their company to make sense of
everything. I'd already experienced hell on earth.

14

PULLING TEETH

I could no longer ignore the shuddering pain of the left side of my face. I couldn't look in the mirror for signs of a spider bite, but I imagined that was what one felt like. It hurt so much that I felt certain it must result in a pretty quick death.

I searched around the humpy for any sign of spider activity, but found nothing, not even a cobweb. Fearing the worst, I lay down on my grass mattress expecting to die.

I'd had enough of this shit. Sitting and waiting for someone to find me in the middle of fucking nowhere seemed pointless. The poison was bound to carry a fatal injection to my head or my heart. I began to say my goodbyes, thinking it was only a matter of time.

My sisters had children I'd never even met before. I hadn't seen one of my sisters for nearly twenty years, all because of a stupid adolescent argument we never resolved. Me and

Mum had only been back in touch for the last couple of years. We were getting on well when we last spoke and there was still plenty of catching up to do.

Lying down in my humpy waiting to die seemed to be taking forever. I spent all day on my back, wondering why there had been no result.

Waiting, waiting, waiting. Waiting to die takes a long time when it doesn't happen.

Pain on a scale I never knew existed was wreaking havoc on me. I had known pain long before being dumped out there, or being bitten by a centipede, but it couldn't compare with what I was experiencing now. The whole left side of my face was aching—throbbing like a hard-on in a nightclub. My neck had swollen up. What the fuck had happened in my sleep for me to deserve this?

If it wasn't a spider and I was still alive the next day, I was going to have to do something drastic about it. The pain in my mouth was grinding me into oblivion. I couldn't tolerate a life in that much pain, no matter how much I wanted to see my family again. I focused all my energy on trying to get to sleep, eventually drifting off to dreamland almost comatose.

* * *

When the sun rose the next morning, I couldn't even open my mouth. It was like my jaw had been wired shut in my sleep. That started me thinking that whatever was wrong with me had more to do with a tooth than a spider.

I was going to have to stick my fingers inside my mouth to trace where it hurt the most, otherwise I wouldn't know the source. Suck 'em in and see what happens.

It took a while, but I finally built up the courage to force my finger inside my locked jaw. I could feel the blisters inside my gums, stretching from my lips to the back of my throat. I traced the most painful route with my finger, shrieking as I did so, trying to discover what was giving me so much grief.

The trail was incredibly painful to follow, with my tongue swollen as well as my gums. My face was that pus-filled, I couldn't even shove a bopple in my mouth. With starvation already hovering, I knew I'd be dead soon if I couldn't eat. It had already been a few days since food last passed my lips.

I knew I had no choice if I wanted to survive. I'd have to bite the bullet and pop the blisters with what tools I had available if I was going to eat again.

So I grabbed for some wire I'd used to skewer the frogs, when they were still around. Clenching my eyes shut, I jammed the wire inside my mouth.

This act of involuntary self-mutilation caused screams of intense pain. I couldn't believe what I was being forced to do to myself. The wire shredded through my skin like my gums were made of dough. It gorged deep, sharp trenches in my aching mouth.

But I couldn't penetrate the bulging blisters, despite my scarily persistent and energetic stabs with the length of wire. They just absorbed each stab and re-inflated with pus. I was left writhing on the floor of my humpy in absolute agony after each jab, unsure what the fuck I could do to break through.

Never one to give up easily, I decided to sharpen one of my car keys on a star picket and have another go. I didn't know if I could bear another failed attempt but my key was so sharp by the time I felt ready that I reckoned I could pierce armour with it.

I had to gee myself up mentally and physically, for the inevitable pain my stabbing would cause. Pulling down my bottom lip, I hacked at the blisters with full ferocity. But again, they refused to pop.

The stench of decay rivalled the pain. I could hardly believe it. Without popping those sacs of pus, I knew I had no chance of getting a grip on the rotten tooth I felt certain was responsible for my agony.

I had no alternative than to ignore the excruciating pain and pump myself up for another go.

Amazingly, this time it worked. The blisters went pop and, in an instant, my mouth filled with putrid black blood and pus.

I nearly threw up. It was as if someone had poured a bag of bad prawns into my mouth and sealed my lips shut.

To get rid of all the crap swilling around in my mouth, I had to literally squeeze the blisters with my fingers and spit the pus out. It was incredible. But, unless I rid myself of the infection, I knew I couldn't eat. I just had to brace myself, or die wondering.

I repeated that process, with the forbearance I had previously summoned when I was carrying mud from the dam bank to my humpy, for the next three or four hours. The stale, pus-filled blood and pus either slithered down the back of my throat, or gathered in pools at my crossed feet.

I knew I shouldn't have swallowed so much of the putrid pus, but at least it had a meaty texture. It had been days since I'd eaten, so I wasn't too upset by the vile taste. Sucking back volumes of black blood, I could feel the poison exiting my body. It was not something I'd choose to digest in normal circumstances, but I had no regrets.

I became desensitised to the pain. I didn't care how much it hurt, really. I just squeezed out the infection between screams. *It hasn't killed me yet, I'm still here!* I knew no matter how much I screamed out in agony, there wouldn't be a reply.

Slowly it began to dawn on me that I would need to extract one of my own teeth. But when I stuck one of my fingers into my mouth, I could feel the jagged insides of my gums. I'd ripped them up so savagely from my stabbing attempts that they oozed from the lacerations.

As soon as I could open my mouth enough to fit more than one finger inside, I felt the offending tooth wiggle. I tried to pull it out but, given that part of the tooth was still attached to my gums, it wasn't going to sever easily. I realised I was going to need a bit more muscle to get the job done.

I crawled out of my humpy for the first time in a few days and went in search of some stronger 12-gauge fencing wire. I'd seen some down at the pump before and felt confident it would do the trick.

It was my first abscess and I couldn't believe one little tooth could cause so much distress. If this was any indication of what they felt like, I wouldn't be putting my hand up for another one in this lifetime.

I knew I'd have to yank it out to alleviate the pain. After finding a suitable thickness of wire near the fence, measuring about 20 centimetres long, I bent it in half in the shape of a pair of pliers.

My crude dentistry tool managed to clasp the offending tooth okay. But no matter how tightly I squeezed it, I couldn't grip with enough force to pull it out.

Grabbing my keys again, I jimmied under the tooth and tried to lever it out. Although it was a mighty painful method, it was mildly effective. That gave me the idea to improve my technique by straightening the wire and bending the end like a hook.

With the hook end wedged under the loose part of my tooth, I could apply maximum pressure on the stubborn attached strands. I used all my remaining physical strength to pull violently on the wire.

I chipped half of another tooth in my first few attempts, which brought on a few more tears. But somehow, after about half an hour of trying, I managed to yank the poisoned pearly white from my gums.

A ripping sound echoed through my humpy as the tooth detached. It was like my own masochistic orchestra. This caused more tears of agony to stream down my face, as a fresh pool of blood and pus and crap oozed from my swollen mouth. It felt worse than watching a food prospect slip through my fingers when I was in the grip of starvation.

* * *

My rotten tooth was undoubtedly my worst experience. It was horrifying. What I had to do to extract that thing still sickens me when I think about it. How does a person do that to themselves?

Although I was rid of the root cause of my pain, I still had the problem of not being able to eat. My jaw still couldn't open properly. I thought I was probably done for, regardless of my sick attempt at dentistry.

Those four days without eating caused me to shed kilos I couldn't afford to cough up. Immune to pain, yet physically drained, what were my chances of making it?

It wasn't as if I had an excess of kilograms to play with. I was starving long before being forced to stop eating and I knew I was in serious trouble.

The pain of chewing still killed me, even when I had the strength to slip a few small bopples into my mouth. But I knew the consequences if I didn't force them down. I didn't have a choice because of my pathetic physical condition.

At least they were only baby bopples, so I didn't really have to chew that hard. I couldn't have handled the agony of shoving down a big juicy one, no matter how delicious it tasted.

Even the pain of moving my lips made me grimace and my energy levels had dwindled to non-existent. The physical effort required to collect food felt beyond my capabilities.

On the fifth day of being confined to my humpy, I decided I'd have to at least try and walk around to see if my legs still worked. I'd become so weak, my legs could hardly carry me. How was I going to collect my bopples when I'd become so feeble?

Almost as soon as I staggered out of my humpy, I stumbled and fell over. I could barely put two steps together. I rolled myself down the dam bank and had a big gulp of water to wash out my bacteria-filled mouth. Then I slithered into the water for a soothing bath.

I used the buoyant support of the water to slowly regain my composure and get to my feet in the dam's shallows. As soon as I took a step on dry ground though, I fell over again. It took an incredible effort just to cover the next 20 metres to reach the fence that surrounded the dam. Once there, I rolled underneath and stumbled out into the paddock for a food run.

Slowly my balance returned, but then my vision started to go. It faded to the point where my eyes were so blurred that I couldn't tell a bopple tree from a blade of grass.

Luckily, I'd covered that ground hundreds of times. I knew my way around the paddock with blinkered vision and managed a few instinctive handfuls of bopples. I shoved down a couple of mouthfuls to re-energise me and shovelled the rest into my pockets for later.

* * *

I'd now spent 71 days in this hell, living for the most part in the humpy I'd built on the top of a dam nearly two months earlier. I wasn't sure exactly how much I had left in me. I'd lost what felt like 60 kilograms and had had to drink my own piss. I'd eaten frogs, caterpillars, leeches, bush berries, grasshoppers, bugs—basically, anything that moved or grew in the dirt—just to keep my heart pulsing.

My world had shrunk to contemplating my next food run and dreaming of a mozzie-free night. Maybe I could live another week or so, or maybe I would die tomorrow—who knew? I'd said goodbye to the people I loved and made peace with myself as I waited for death to arrive.

On that day when my luck finally turned around, I'd emerged from my humpy to collect some water in the morning, as usual, before retreating to its shelter until the late afternoon. It was pretty windy that particular day and I'd spent hours just listening for signs of a miracle and watching my curtains flap in the breeze.

By late afternoon I was immersed in my usual routine of preparing for my daily food collection. Staring at the sinking sun, counting the last rays before it was time to scamper out for another desperate daily food run.

Two or three times throughout that afternoon I thought I'd heard a car. Once upon a time I would have jumped out of my humpy and scanned the horizon, desperate for any glimpse of a dust cloud trail or maybe a chopper, but now from past experience I just assumed it was the wind and drifted off into semi-consciousness again.

I didn't even get too excited when a purr stirred me from my slumber—it might be a diesel engine, maybe the sound of a four-wheel drive coming towards me. The wind howling through my humpy sometimes simulated the sound of a vehicle, so I thought it might have been playing tricks on me again.

By this time my energy level was really very low. I figured: if it really is someone, surely they'll at least come and check out my humpy. You don't just drive past a big pile of mud on the top of a dam, with a cattle trough as its roof, without having a look inside, do you? Not with a makeshift cross made out of sticks marking the spot above for added emphasis.

I could guarantee it wasn't here the last time anyone drove past. It served as a solemn symbol of my fate and also reminded the world that someone lived inside, religious or not.

Again I heard through the curtains the chug of something resembling a motor. And then it was quickly followed by a sound I could hardly believe.

A gear change! I heard a fucking gear change! And, given that wind doesn't change gears, it finally hit me like a bolt of lightning that whatever was coming down the road was my ticket out of there.

I'm saved! I'm bloody saved!

Rushing outside my humpy, energised by the prospect of being rescued, I was met by the sight of a four-wheel drive, with two young guys upfront, making a beeline straight towards me. I jumped out at them, waving my hands like a man possessed and thanking God for everything He'd given me, while urgently signalling for them to stop.

I couldn't believe it. After all this time I wasn't exactly sure, but I thought I'd been waiting for someone to come along for pretty close to three months. I had hardly absorbed this incredible twist in my fate before new thoughts began rushing through my racing brain. They were stopping, for sure, but what would I do next?

There were a few possessions I wanted to take with me, wherever I ended up alive all of a sudden. Like my poisoned tooth and the car keys I'd carried all this way. They were up the far end of the humpy and really hard to reach. Unless I crawled back inside, it seemed like my remnants would have to stay there.

To overcome this difficulty, I attempted to hook them by using the bits of wire I'd previously set aside for drying out the frogs I ate for lunch. As the two bewildered station hands drove towards me in their four-wheel drive, all they could see was my bottom half poking out of my makeshift home.

My life had come down to these few basic objects of despair. They were so important to me that I risked being overlooked or shot retrieving them, but I was determined not to leave them behind.

I didn't have enough energy left to stretch out fully towards where they were. But the adrenaline coursing through my veins was enough to get the job done; my heart beat hard against my thin chest as I reeled them in.

My mind rushed as the Land Cruiser turned into the paddock. I scrambled to my feet and started waving wildly at my unknown rescuers with my free hand, but I couldn't make a sound to save my life. I tried to scream out to them, but I was voiceless—my words dried up as soon as I uttered them.

They pulled up about a hundred metres or so away from me, just as I scooped up the last of my meagre belongings. I was eager to thank whoever had found me at last.

It would be fair to assume that the two station hands in the four-wheel drive—Taz and Bruce from Birrindudu Station—must have been a bit hesitant when they first got a good look at me. For them it was meant to be just another day at their bloody big office; they only stopped at the dam as an afterthought, because they were in that corner of the station and didn't want to come back all this way in the furthest corner of the furthest paddock again for a while. Because of that decision they found they had a wild man looking back at them.

They later told me that their first instinct, when they looked up from the track and saw my crumpled figure crawling out of my humpy, was that I was a dingo rustling through a turkey's nest. They contemplated reaching for the gun in the back to put me out of my misery, but hesitated as I waved my arms at them.

It must have looked pretty strange to Taz and Bruce to see this wiry ferret of a thing diving in and out of the humpy. They could have been excused if they'd thought I was some kind of crazy nutter scratching around for a shotgun of my own and pumped some lead into me.

As they drew closer they realised I was actually a human being, albeit an incredibly scrawny one, who looked like he hadn't had a decent feed in the last century, but as though he had just won the lottery.

A skeleton of a thing with a straggly beard and nothing but a pair of tattered shorts hanging off me for clothing, I tried running towards them. But I only managed to fall flat on my face in the dirt, going nowhere fast.

Quickly rising to my feet again, in case they vanished like a mirage, I staggered down the dam bank a few more steps before tumbling into the earth again and again. My clumsiness was overshadowed by feeling so delirious at the amazing prospect of being found alive.

By now the boys could tell I was no more of a threat to them than the cowshit on the bottom of their boots and they jumped out of the vehicle to help. Still parked a safe distance away, they yelled out as they made their way to me from across the paddock: 'Are you all right there, mate?'

When I replied that I was glad to see them, they could not have appreciated how much I meant it. I couldn't speak louder than a whisper at full scream when I blabbered those first words, but they could at least see that I was trying to communicate. Finally I could talk to someone.

Bruce had been the first outline I had made out, sitting behind the wheel of the Cruiser. He appeared to be in his late twenties and loomed large at about six foot tall, with the typical appearance of a hardy stockman. With his cowboy hat covering his mat of black hair and his Wrangler jeans dripping off him, he looked like he had stepped straight out of the movies, albeit a little hesitantly.

Taz was much shorter and stockier than Bruce, and seemed to be aged in his late teens or early twenties. Clad in pretty much the same outfit as his mate, he stood back a couple of steps, completely flummoxed by what, or who, confronted him.

Both of them seemed to be in disbelief that someone was actually living out there, but they quickly understood my desperation—it was etched in my face and echoed in the bones poking out of my emaciated body. They asked me what the bloody hell I was doing out there, but I didn't know where to start.

It had been so long since I'd last conversed with a real person—more than two months since I'd spoken to anyone besides myself or God or the dingoes. My words were spilling out of my mouth faster than my mind could process them.

'You wouldn't believe it. I was dumped out here and left for dead by a bunch of blackfellas. I've spent the past few months wandering through the desert eating frogs and lizards and whatever else I could find to stay alive. Dingoes have been stalking me; I've been living on grass. Thank God you're here.'

The boys looked stunned and figured they'd better fire back a few questions to determine the extent of my sanity. For starters, they asked me what day I thought it was. I told them that, to the best of my knowledge, it was 14 April but I'd kind of lost track of stuff and could be out by a few days.

'It's the fourth of April,' they said, before asking how long I'd been stuck out there.

'I'm not sure exactly the number of days, but it's been a while,' I bounced back. 'I was hijacked on the twenty-fourth of January.'

They looked up and down my puny frame in pure astonishment and the air between us fell silent for a moment.

Taz had spent his whole life in the outback and reckoned he wouldn't survive for four days out here on his own, regardless of how much grass there was to eat. But, from the look of me, he thought I wasn't far off being three months without a decent feed.

The boys gently reached out to usher me to the padded comfort of the Cruiser. How could I explain to them in a few simple sentences that just getting to this sweet moment had all but killed me.

15
WHAT'S FOR DINNER?

It felt so surreal to be sitting in a vehicle with real people to talk to after Taz and Bruce finally rescued me. The boys couldn't believe how pathetic I looked—it was hard enough to believe myself.

Being just skin and bone, the ride back to the station house felt pretty bloody uncomfortable. The sharp angles of my emaciated body ground into the ute's upholstery as we negotiated the lumpy track back to the Boree intersection. Still, I wasn't complaining. It served as a stark reminder of how close to death from starvation I'd actually come.

The only real negative about being plucked from the desert in the late afternoon by Taz and Bruce was being so fucking hungry. I was just about to go on a food run when they found me and my stomach couldn't help but grumble about their timing.

It was about a 45-minute drive to the station and the boys promised I'd have a decent feed in my stomach before the hour was up. A gutful of sausages was better than a handful of bopples any day, they reckoned. I was keen to eat anything that didn't come fresh from the ground, with the dirt and caterpillars still attached.

They offered me a drink from the water bottle that was sitting on the floor of the Cruiser and I took a hearty swig, but it was hot and tasted like shit. Thanks but no thanks, boys.

After seven weeks of slurping on God's own pure drops of goodness from the dam, I wasn't particularly keen to gulp down boiled crap from a sweaty bottle. Especially when I could be sucking on a strawberry milkshake in a matter of minutes. That and hamburgers were what I'd been dreaming of and for once those dreams looked like coming true.

I poked at the boys a few times as we were driving back to the station house, just to make sure I wasn't hallucinating. But they were certainly for real. I finally felt as if everything would be okay, as long as I had them next to me for reassurance.

There wasn't much chit-chat between us as we meandered to the Boree intersection and turned left for the final stretch to civilisation. I struggled to comprehend the enormity of my rescue and the boys seemed stunned by what they had stumbled on.

At the intersection I looked across at where I'd made my SOS out of rocks. I told the boys about it but they said no one had noticed them and I figured the grass had buried the rocks from the sky over the months.

Catching a glimpse of myself in the rear-vision mirror after we pulled up to open a gate, I gave out a petrified yelp. I'd stopped looking at my reflection in the dam weeks earlier as my health and outlook sharply deteriorated. The hairy, straggly beast now staring back at me in no way resembled what I remembered of my former self.

My appearance had given the boys as much of a fright as I'd just given myself, but this distraction was only momentary. I regained my composure with the knowledge I wasn't going to get any skinnier.

Slowly we made our way up the driveway of the station house and Taz and Bruce began to prepare for my arrival. To see a real home brought me to the brink of tears.

As soon as the Cruiser stopped, both Taz and Bruce jumped out and ran in different directions. They told me to stay in my seat, promising that everything would be okay.

I was the last person they had to explain that to, after 71 days lost in the middle of nowhere. I felt quite content to park my bony arse against the Cruiser and wait for the cavalry to arrive.

* * *

Food had been the first thing on my mind when we finally pulled up at the homestead. There were a few formalities to go through—like talking to doctors and the police—but my stomach was my top priority.

Leigh, the station nurse, was the first person to come hurrying out to check me over. The look on her face was one of pure fear—I could tell she'd never set eyes on such a wasted human being and that came as no surprise. I'm sure there are not too many people, if anyone, who have lived through what I'd just endured.

Taz and Bruce re-emerged from the homestead and wouldn't let me walk into the house unaided. They sort of carried me inside and plumped me down on one of the nice comfy couches that filled the spacious lounge room.

As people buzzed around me, calling police and doctors and Christ knows who else, I gently reminded them that I was bloody starving. Even a bowl of bopples would satisfy me, but I'd love a plate of sausages.

Leigh was horrified by that suggestion, explaining that I'd have to be weaned back on to solid foods before indulging in a serve of meat. With no energy to argue, I made do with a tin of fruit. Food out of a can had never tasted so good.

The doctors were the first people to be called on the phone once we were inside the station house. Someone rang the hospital at Katherine, the closest town, and the nearby Kalkaringi health clinic.

The medical fraternity weren't quite sure how to take me. For obvious reasons no one had ever considered how to respond to a phone call asking for advice on how to deal with a shadow of a man in the depths of starvation. Everyone was in a bit of a tizz and I felt overawed simply to be alive.

All of a sudden Ricky Megee had become important to someone. I wasn't just a figment of my own imagination—I was a real person who mattered to other human beings. To top it off, the people at the station were so warm towards me—I wished I'd seen their caring faces two months before.

After the doctors were spoken to, it was time to call the police. That conversation ended up being a sudden return to reality, as I seemed to be more of a hindrance than someone who desperately needed help.

The cops suggested I drive the two hours back to Kalkaringi and make a statement. After months of staggering through the desert, shedding 60 kilograms in the process, I didn't much feel like putting in the overtime. Instead I sat back on the couch, glad I hadn't been relying on them to save me in the first place.

Talking to the cops about my attempted murder didn't seem as important as food at that point. I was in no hurry to go anywhere and felt sure that at least the doctors had plans for me. I was just happy to be alive and was more interested in what my options were on the food front—not what my next move would be.

It was quite peaceful there at the homestead surrounded by such good people. I could never thank them enough and their generosity will remain with me forever.

Leigh the station nurse was understandably worried about what I could and couldn't eat—she didn't want to let me pig out too much without the okay from a doctor. But once the initial fluster was over and done with and I'd eaten up my tinned fruit, Kathleen, the station cook, went to work on a big container of pumpkin soup.

I didn't ask for it, but pumpkin soup is my favourite. I reckoned Kathleen had thrown the whole patch on the stove for my troubles.

It was a bloody big container Leigh came back with for me anyway—and it tasted delicious. I've got my own recipes for pumpkin soup, but this one was better than any I've ever tasted and I ate the whole bowl.

Eating big portions of food I didn't have to collect for myself felt a bit strange to start with. I was so used to simple mouthfuls of bopples and spriggie-spriggies—especially in the later weeks when my food sources reached a low. It took a while for it to sink in that I could swallow repeated mouthfuls virtually effort-free.

My teeth were still sore from the abscess—I couldn't open my mouth or chew properly, courtesy of my aching jaw—but I gave it a go. It was home-made soup after all, and well worth the effort.

I convinced Leigh to throw in a couple of slices of bread for good measure. She was kind enough to oblige—even though she still wasn't sure what I should be eating.

With a good meal in my stomach, it came time to let people know I was still breathing. To get the ball rolling, I called my sister Tina in Brisbane.

As soon as she answered the phone and realised who it was, she started crying—which started me off as well. I'm not the type of guy to cry on the phone normally, but I couldn't help it. The sense of relief overwhelmed both of us.

I didn't really say much to Tina about what I had endured. I just told her I was alive after being dumped and lost for 70-odd days in the desert and that I loved her—everything was going to be all right.

I couldn't believe I was speaking to a familiar person—finally, someone who knew me for who I was.

Tina had gathered I was missing. A few people had phoned her up in the previous months looking for me and she made some calls to find out if anyone had seen me. Obviously no one had, and she feared for the worst. But she didn't tell Mum because she didn't want to worry her.

The truth is, Tina had no theory as to what could have happened to me. She had no idea of where I was and no inkling of what to do about it.

It was so good to hear her voice on the other end of the line, though—I couldn't wait for the moment to see my first familiar face.

Getting back to reality came with a few surprises, but having a shower was probably the biggest shock. The boys found me some clothes to wear—I couldn't really step back into my filthy, ripped shorts. I felt super keen for a shower to scrub off all the ingrained dirt.

I wasn't expecting a full body mirror, though. I almost walked straight into my skeletal remains. *Holy hell, holy hell, holy bloody hell—look at me!*

The bigger the mirror, the greater the horror. I'd seen my face in the rear-vision mirror on the way to the homestead and that had stopped me in my tracks, but this seemed completely unreal. *What the bloody hell is that?*

My screams of shock alerted Leigh and she ran in to the bathroom to see what the problem was. I couldn't see myself; I didn't see myself. Who the hell was that staring back at me in that big bright mirror? I felt terrified.

Meaning no disrespect to the men and women who fought and died for our country, it looked like I'd miraculously escaped from a prisoner-of-war camp. Leigh assured me that everything was okay. It was only a reflection—being alive was more important.

With Leigh's reassurance, I stepped into the shower cubicle hesitantly. I had not been capable of standing up in the one spot for long for weeks and asked Leigh to put a chair in the shower for me.

The hot water running down my back felt so good. I sat there for what felt like hours fiddling with the taps as the water washed over me—choosing the ideal mix of hot and cold water was not something I'd had to think about for a long while.

Sitting there with my eyes firmly closed, I started to drift back to the isolation of my humpy. I couldn't feel the water any longer—I was just lying back next to my dam as if I'd imagined my rescue. For a good five minutes I sat there confused—could I really be having a shower in a real house, or was this another bad dream?

I'd already eaten food I didn't have to collect myself for dinner and I was now experiencing a hot shower—yet I didn't feel all that different. The surrealness of my new environment left me in a state of pure shock. If I wasn't having a shower, I'd be trying to steal some sleep without being attacked by mozzies, wondering when I would die.

I opened my eyes and touched the walls of the shower recess—this was the real thing all right. It was time to rejoin the human race.

Afterwards Taz and Bruce came over to Leigh and her partner Greg's cottage where I was staying, to see how I was doing. I felt normal for a change, sitting there having a yarn about how the hell we all ended up in the one spot.

We finished up with a few happy snaps of us all together before the boys went back to their own cottages for the night. They had another long day ahead of them and left me sitting back on the lounge, not quite sure what to think.

One minute I was preparing to go on a food run and the next I was scoffing pumpkin soup. I had a beer in one hand, a rolled smoke in the other, sitting back on a comfy couch watching Greg flip through his impressive selection of country music. So much for giving up smoking.

We turned our attention to the television for a while, but I couldn't say what was on. I felt stunned—politely oblivious to others.

Faced with early-morning responsibilities, Greg and Leigh went to bed while I stayed up clunking about the house, touching things. I'd open the fridge door just to have a look at it with the light on—staring open-mouthed at all that food sitting in there. All I had to do was pick something out and throw it on a pan and I'd be eating again.

Leigh came out to keep me company for a while. Then I managed to sneak in a couple of hours' rest on a bed supported by a real mattress—no grass fluffing required.

The next morning Greg got up for work some time before six. Leigh cooked us all up a big breakfast to get the day rolling—bacon, eggs, tomatoes, she didn't hold back. I soaked it all up, knowing that in a couple of hours the doctors would be there to end the peace.

16

INTO THE FRYING PAN

Once the doctors arrived on the tarmac, it was all systems go. I said goodbye to Leigh and climbed up the stairs of the plane, wondering how I'd react. There were bound to be plenty of questions asked about how I'd survived for so long and I wasn't sure how to respond.

There were two doctors on board with me and they didn't muck around getting to work—we weren't even up in the air before they'd put a drip in. Looking at me, they couldn't believe I was alive—let alone alert.

They were most concerned to find out whether my liver was bad or functioning properly. I seemed to be passing all the medical tests they gave me and the urgency of their efforts began to subside. But then a new problem arose.

Just before we arrived in Katherine, an hour or so away, traffic controllers informed the pilot by radio that the local hospital was being evacuated. Rising floodwaters were threatening their outback township.

After all I'd gone through, what were the chances of this? Typical of my luck really—I finally get found and the hospital floods.

As they had to evacuate the entire hospital, we landed in Katherine to pick up a few of the sicker patients to taxi to Darwin.

* * *

It was pretty hectic at the Darwin Hospital. There were all those extra patients to deal with and the busy staff gave me an initial assessment and promptly forgot about me. They left me alone on a trolley in a hallway, while heaps of medical staff buzzed about, frantically wondering what to do with the influx from Katherine.

My ambitions remained the same as when Taz and Bruce found me—all I wanted to do was eat. I convinced an orderly who kept walking past to get me some food. He only had to take one look at me to tell how hungry I was. He'd seen me lying on the trolley for long enough to assume I needed him to raid the kitchen for me.

I'm not sure where he went, but he came through with a big plate of sandwiches. I ended up spending all night in the hallway and my new orderly mate kept feeding me. The next day they found me a temporary room, before moving me into a general ward where I stayed for the best part of two weeks.

We were next to the rehabilitation ward, which they locked up each night to stop the alcoholics and drug addicts from walking around the hospital and freaking out the other patients. Besides watching television, there wasn't a lot to do to pass the time in hospital. All my tests were positive and it seemed only my weight was a worry to the doctors.

My body had pulled through with nothing more than wear and tear—besides my extreme weight loss. I looked bad, but my organs were functioning well.

I just put my internal resilience down to being so healthy before I was dumped. I was as solid as a rock back then and had no intention of letting any hiccup stop me.

During my first days in hospital, it wasn't unusual for me to have twelve meals in 24 hours. But my healthy appetite caused a few dramas. My hospital room was like a little supermarket inside. I was eating every hour on the hour, but hardly sleeping because I was suffering repeated nightmares of being stuck out there again. I'd wake up shuddering from the possibility, unable to shake the images of desertion from my head.

* * *

When I was in my late teens and moved up to Queensland, I sort of lost contact with my mum. I'd ring her occasionally, just to let her know I was still alive, but she found it hard to keep track of me. I was always moving house or changing my phone number. Our calls became less and less regular, and then somehow we didn't speak for ten years.

Then I got back in touch with her again a couple of years back and we've been pretty good since then. I spoke to her three or four times over the Christmas just before I disappeared and saw her a couple of weeks into January.

I told her that I'd got a job interstate and was leaving Brisbane and she told me to keep in touch. After not hearing from me for a few months, she wasn't too alarmed. Mum was used to the gaps in our contact.

When my sister Tina first rang Mum at home in Queensland to say they'd found me, she didn't know what Tina was talking about. 'What do you mean—they've found Ricky? Found him where?' she asked. 'Is he all right?'

It was the first Mum had heard that I was a missing person. She says now that within herself she'd felt like something was wrong. It didn't occur to her that I might have disappeared, but it was strange because I'd been keeping in touch pretty regularly for the past couple of years.

She later told me: 'To hear you'd been found like that, my heart just died. I didn't recognise you really when I saw the photos in the newspaper—the awful state you were in. No one wants to see their son like that.'

When Mum first called me at the hospital, we didn't say much. She said I sounded really lethargic. There were a few tears and she said she wanted to come up and see me. But she couldn't afford it and in any case I reckoned she was better off at home—I'd made it this far on my own. I felt pretty sure I could handle hospital and it would have only stressed her out seeing me like that.

When my sister Tina arrived in Darwin not long after, one of the first things I did was give her a big shopping list of food. I could keep it stashed in the cupboard until the coast was clear for me to gamma-ray it in the microwave.

Tins of baked beans, party pies, pizza—whatever fitted on the microwave tray could fit in my stomach. You could say everyone was happier for it. I wasn't annoying the nurses for more food each time they came around the ward and no one was bothering me.

It really helped in my recovery having Tina around for those few days. We've had our moments over the years, but she's as close to me as anyone and she was someone familiar I could talk to about my transformation. But then she had to get back home to look after her daughter and it was up to me to take care of my own hunger.

I spoke to Mum again and started getting calls from more and more familiar voices. Some people hadn't known I was missing until I'd been found. Others hadn't heard from me for ages and assumed something had gone pear-shaped.

Eating was my comfort—it made me feel normal again. I never experienced any pains or cramps from eating so much—I just couldn't get enough food. The doctors didn't understand that all the food in the hospital couldn't feed my appetite. Just to be eating real food again—food I didn't have to catch myself—and having access to a microwave was a pleasure they could never comprehend.

But I didn't want to just sit on my bum eating all day. I'd go for little walks around the perimeter of the hospital—up and down the steps to try and build up the muscles in my legs. Even that limited amount of exercise was an effort. I'd be left sprawled on the bed exhausted afterwards, wondering why I kept pushing myself so hard.

There were no bopples to collect in that concrete jungle—just diseases.

I wanted to put weight on straight away and not lose the plot mentally, but they weren't making it easy. Ten to fifteen times a day I'd be traipsing up and down the hallway to heat up whatever I could get my hands on. I soon got sick of that. To avoid having to hobble down the corridor and pester the nurses so often for a snack, I eventually just snatched the communal microwave. When everyone else in the ward fell asleep, I stashed it under my bed for regular and easy access.

As long as I could get the microwave back before the nurses changed shift in the morning, I could have all the food I wanted at my fingertips through the night. I kept it under the bed and carried it back hidden under a trolley early each day. No one was any the wiser and I felt much healthier for my efforts. There were two microwaves in the kitchen anyway—it wasn't as if I was depriving anyone else who felt like a midnight snack.

'Are you still eating?!' the nurses would exclaim. 'The doctors said you're not allowed to have so much food.' *Of course I'm still eating—look at me—I'm starving.*

One morning I didn't wake up in time, though. My microwave-borrowing plan came completely unstuck. I could hear the head nurse doing the rounds and everyone talking about the microwave. It was still under my bed at that stage, so I hid it in the cupboard and threw a blanket over the top.

During a search of my room they uncovered the microwave and a box of jam spreads I'd grabbed from the kitchen when the staff weren't looking. How ironic could life be? When I was finally rescued from certain death, the doctors didn't want me to eat. Even when I felt so hungry, they were afraid it could cause internal damage.

But the more doctors told me not to, the more I wanted to eat. I reckoned my body would've let me know if I had been eating too much. The more food I shoved in my mouth, the better I felt—and, until the docs had solid evidence to the contrary, I wasn't about to stop.

Now I was being accused of stealing a microwave and hoarding stolen packets of jam. Why was I borrowing the microwave? I didn't know if anyone had noticed, but I'd spent 71 days in the desert and lost 60 kilograms. I was fucking starving.

Words were exchanged but no charges were laid and I checked out of hospital pretty soon afterwards. I made my way back into society on my own two compression-bandaged feet.

But where did I fit in society and what did I feel like for lunch? They were both questions that couldn't be answered immediately. At least now the only ribs that concerned me were served on a plate with a side of chips and a cold beer.

17

CSI TERRITORY

Police from the Major Crime Unit came to see me pretty soon after I arrived in Darwin Hospital.

Detective Jason Bradbury was very polite and keen to hear what I had to say. He sounded like he wanted to do something about it and trace the events leading up to my being left for dead, so those responsible could be brought to justice.

The period between when I picked up the hitchhiker and woke up in the hole was the hardest to remember. I didn't need much reminding of the next ten weeks, but my memories of the hours that led up to me being dumped were fragmented due to the effects of being drugged.

The strongest of my hazy memories from that period was of me fighting someone for my car. I remember how I had realised that it wouldn't start because it was bogged up to the axles. There were people searching through my vehicle while I looked on helplessly.

How that explained where I ended up, I didn't know. Obviously I didn't put myself in the hole and try to starve myself to death in the desert in the middle of the wet season. Someone had some explaining to do.

I was very honest with the cops from the start, but during the interviews I left bits out that I couldn't be sure of because I didn't want to tell them things I myself wasn't convinced were true. At that time I wasn't sure about what details I knew as fact, and what I thought had happened but wasn't clear about yet.

After checking out of hospital, I called the police from Major Crime to try and help them piece together what had happened to me. They picked me up from where I was staying in the suburb of Fannie Bay and brought me in to the city for an official interview.

It was here I met Senior Sergeant Wendy Schultz. She was a big, no-nonsense cop who reckoned she believed me. She just wanted to go over a few details that didn't add up to her.

I'd been honest with the police from the start about my own criminal history. I told them where I was coming from and going to. Then, all of a sudden, they wanted to turn that information against me.

I walked out of that first official interview with Senior Sergeant Schultz wondering what I was getting myself in for. How could I trust her to conduct a thorough criminal investigation, if the focus of that investigation was going to be me? What about the people responsible for my attempted murder?

The next interview with her occurred out at police headquarters at Berrimah a few days later. Now she really had a go, accusing me of everything from impersonating a federal police officer in Brisbane to being a drug runner. She threw a police file in front of me as thick as an encyclopaedia. I'd only ever been done for relatively minor convictions a long time in the past, but she questioned my involvement in all sorts of fanciful conspiracies.

'Maybe you were having a drug flashback, Rick, and you imagined the whole thing. What do you think about that scenario? Or else you were on a drug run—what do you think about that?'

None of her accusations could be supported. It was just bullshit based on what disgruntled cops in another lifetime had scribbled down in notes on my police file, for reasons apparent only to their active imaginations.

Slumped in a chair in her police interview room, I weighed no more than 55 kilograms and didn't have the energy to defend myself. She could make up as many stories as she liked—it didn't alter the fact that someone dumped me in a hole and left me to die in the desert. It also didn't help them find my vehicle, which was still planted in the dirt somewhere off the Buntine Highway.

Fucking idiot is what I thought—but I didn't say anything. I still wanted to cooperate with her, in the hope she would do something to catch the people who tried to kill me. And it wasn't hard for her to intimidate me, given my current physical condition.

I was in the dark about what had happened and who was responsible, as much as she was. Yet she kept throwing baseless accusations at me—she was on a useless fishing expedition. It appeared as though only one of us was interested in the identity of my attempted murderers. If whoever was responsible only knew who they were dealing with, they might have realised they couldn't kill me so easily in the first place.

I'd told the cops as much as I could remember about the circumstances. That included where I thought the car was. I gave them a good description of the hitchhiker I'd picked up, who I believed had drugged me.

Wherever I'd ploughed my car into the scrub, I knew it wouldn't have moved because it was bogged up to the axles. From what I could remember, it was about half a kilometre off the Buntine Highway, somewhere between Kalkaringi and Halls Creek. I didn't know which side of the road it was on because I didn't know what direction I was driving when I headed off-road. I would have peeled off anywhere in an attempt to shake my unwelcome passenger.

Finally, I'd had enough of their interrogations. I aimed a few questions of my own at them. 'How about you stop getting into me for five seconds, and tell me what the fuck you've been doing to find my car? Have you even been looking for it?'

'We are, mate, we are. Calm down. We've got two choppers and a fixed-wing aircraft flying up and down sections of the Buntine. It's only a matter of time before we find it.'

I was starting to doubt myself with all their hysterical theories. Who did they think I was and what was I supposedly doing out there in the first place if I wasn't telling the truth? They could have checked with Centrelink in Port Hedland, where I had a job waiting for me, if they'd wanted to know what my intentions were. Doing a mate a favour by driving his kid to Adelaide wasn't a crime.

I hadn't been in trouble with the police for more than eight years. They could go on all they liked about what kind of person I supposedly was, but it wasn't doing much to find out who tried to kill me. I'd even given them a description of the hitchhiker. But they chose not to release it to the media, in the belief they could find him quicker themselves on the quiet.

It became obvious they placed little value on what I had to say. I decided if they didn't want to follow through with the information I'd provided, I needed to do something myself.

My doctor suggested hypnotherapy as a possible method to help revive my memory of the events leading up to being dumped. He gave me a couple of numbers to call—these were people he knew who had been effective in the past helping date-rape victims.

I rang one and made an appointment. Although I remained sceptical of how helpful a hypnotherapist could be for me, I went into the session with an open mind, in the belief that some good might come of it. Hypnotherapy is not something I'd believe in normally. But I was at the point where I'd try anything if it helped me remember how I ended up in that hole.

It was a strange thing to have done, being hypnotised. The therapist just started talking and talking and talking, about all sorts of things that seemed irrelevant. The next thing I knew I was out to it. The best way I could describe it is like being bored to sleep when you're still wide awake.

Once I was under his spell, he started prompting me to remember elements of my abduction I didn't think were possible to unlock. It was a bit frightening how vividly I could see things all of a sudden. Over the next couple of nights, more and more of those memories came flooding back to me.

They didn't feel like dreams—I could literally feel myself there again, and picture my surroundings and those around me in minute detail.

Over the following weeks the memories stalked me. Without warning, I'd have a flashback of a conversation I had with one of my captors. It felt like he was standing right next to me.

The faces—I could see them all clearly and knew what they were saying, on the few occasions they did speak to me. They were searching through my vehicle for something, but I didn't know what and they wouldn't tell me.

Later on, I told the cops I'd had some hypnotherapy sessions and remembered a lot more about how it all happened and who was involved. They seemed interested and asked me to come in and see them.

All the pieces of the puzzle were adding up in my cleared head. I now knew some of the missing links in the attempt on my life. I could now be certain all three of the blackfellas I'd stopped to help were involved, among others.

Yet it seemed the cops preferred to believe that I'd taken a bad acid trip or something, and put myself in the desert. Despite the mounting evidence to the contrary.

I didn't even bother telling them that I had another mate who lived out that way who was aware of what had happened to me. He called from a remote town one afternoon to ask why some blackfella was walking around in my $400 jacket, the one I bought in Canada. My mate knew it was my jacket because of its distinctive colour and fabric. He found it strange for a community blackfella to be wearing something similar, so he followed him home.

The jacket was in the back of my car when I was rolled, so I knew the person wearing it had to be involved. I added the thieving bastard to the list of people who had some explaining to do.

It had been hard to temper my anger towards the people who tried to kill me. But, due to the unwillingness of police to investigate for whatever reason, they were going to get away with it.

It is something that will eat me from the inside out if I let it. I have to walk away and exact my revenge by living a happy and successful life—despite their attempts to knock me off.

When I was first dumped, I was filled with rage for the people who put me there. Even though I didn't know who they were, I plotted my revenge.

Even when I was dying of thirst and starvation, my thoughts turned to sorting out whoever did that to me. I planned to get back to civilisation, organise some money, have a hamburger and a strawberry milkshake, and find the low-life who'd fucked me up. I'd see how they liked being dumped in a hole in the desert. If they were lucky, they'd receive an exploding envelope laced with anthrax in the mail.

But as my chances of surviving weakened, so did my need for revenge. As the weeks of wandering aimlessly through the parched landscape wore on, I re-evaluated a lot of my philosophies in life. Seeing the people who'd left me to die suffer didn't seem to matter so much any more.

It didn't really worry me what people thought or believed about what had happened to me. I was living and breathing evidence that what I said was true, and no one could take that away.

I wanted justice and the truth. I wanted to know myself what really happened and have whoever was responsible brought before the courts and punished. And I wanted to achieve those aims without violence.

Now it seems it will be a matter for me or karma to deal with. I'd prefer karma to work its magic.

Not surprisingly, station hands found my car two months after I was found and roughly where I told the cops to look. It was in the same damaged condition I told the police it would be—with some of my belongings missing, as I expected. But still they had doubted my story.

Had the cops conducted an aerial grid search of the Buntine Highway as they told me they were going to do, my car would have been spotted easily. I didn't bother arguing that point with them.

Yet there it was—one Mitsubishi Challenger, found bogged up to the axles 1.6 kilometres south of the Buntine Highway. Found on a cattle station adjoining the one where I was plucked from near the Northern Territory–West Australian border.

The car was a bit further off the highway than I thought I had driven. But then, I had been driving with my windscreen caved in and a blackfella in the back seat who kept on punching me in the head. I could understand the slight inaccuracy regarding distance.

When the Challenger was found, its windows were smashed, my wallet and two phones were missing, my passport wasn't in there, some of my tools were gone and apparently all my other belongings were scattered about inside, so the cops told me. I'm not sure if my boots were still in the back, but all of a sudden my car was a crime scene.

Who knows what they pulled out of there. They did some forensic testing, they tell me. I've heard nothing of the results. But I know what happened and so do the people who tried to kill me.

Now that it's all done and dusted, I have no desire to hunt them down. Everything changed for me out there. My revenge on them is being alive and making a success of the rest of my life.

A life of crime and violence is one I left behind a long time ago. It's not a place I want to revisit in a hurry.

Still, they will never be quite sure if and when Big Rick might come around looking to collect. That's their karma.

* * *

Despite my requests to them, Northern Territory police chose not to be interviewed for this book, nor to comment officially on the status of their investigation.

18

FROM THE DOCTORS' MOUTHS

While the Northern Territory police were tight-lipped and unwilling to say anything on the record about my case, I found two doctors who were happy to discuss their wildly differing opinions. Here is the very candid assessment of Dr Len Notaras, Director of Medical Services at Royal Darwin Hospital:

> I was aware of Ricky's case from the time he was retrieved and taken to Katherine Hospital. I knew he had an unusual story, somewhere between adventure and unbelievable.
>
> It was important to remember that, whatever the circumstances that had led to his condition, here was a man who was previously over 100 kilograms and he now weighed just 46. I can understand on that level that something significant happened to Ricky. His story

was an incredible adventure in terms of how he got there, but his claims raised more questions than solved answers.

They were reasonable claims. Nothing is impossible, so it's not impossible to believe what he says he did. What is hard is to join the dots, to believe that he spent that amount of time out there after being hijacked by folk he tried to help. It's quite plausible, but I don't know if he did or he didn't do the things he says.

Physically he was not unlike the victims of Changi when he first came to hospital. I think one of the young lads who found him commented he looked like a prisoner of war, like a walking skeleton. Obviously he must have been somewhere for a prolonged period because that sort of weight loss just doesn't happen overnight. In his favour he built a makeshift humpy in the middle of nowhere that was close to fresh water.

With a water supply and shelter he would have gone a long way to giving himself a chance to survive. If he ate frogs and lizards and whatever else he could capture, his food source could be constant as well. But he would have survived for only a very short period without water.

In normal conditions humans need 600 millilitres to a litre of water minimum every day to avoid dehydration. In the desert you would need up to 3 or 4 litres every day to meet those same requirements. If you didn't have a litre a day you would die very quickly, probably the first day.

In biblical times of course Christ walked into the desert for 40 days and 40 nights without food so there are historical precedents for not eating. Ricky obviously spent a lot longer in the desert and had water and shelter. His huge amount of weight loss might explain why he came in to hospital with such confused stories. The fact his thoughts were somewhat jumbled doesn't surprise me; anyone who spent that long in the desert would be.

Just recently Mexican fishermen survived adrift at sea for eight months and, if their stories are accurate, they lived on nothing but raw fish and birds the whole time. It sounds impossible but it's not. The Thredbo disaster showed us that you can survive being trapped in extreme circumstances and that's been proven in other cases around the world.

His electrolytes, or biochemistry levels, were remarkably stable when he was brought to hospital. I discussed his condition with the hospital's senior clinicians and they were happy with him overall—he appeared to have suffered no long-term damage. If he went out as a fit man, with knowledge of the bush, it's possible his story could come down on the side of credible. The SAS are well-known bushmen as well and have proven you could survive for that long in the desert and lose less weight.

I've seen a lot of things in the Territory that I would not expect to see anywhere else and this is another example. There was a strange case a few years ago where a man tried to slowly poison his wife with paracetamol at one of the remote communities; and then there's the mystery that still surrounds the Falconio case. In lots of these cases it's hard to put together what actually happened, but they all show the Territory is different.

Seeing Ricky's recovery was just as incredible as seeing how emaciated he was to start with. As with prisoners of war, we had to be careful with his recovery and try and get him to gradually put weight back on; otherwise it could put stress on his vital organs. But Ricky just wanted to eat. He certainly has the constitution of someone who is very fit; he responded well to treatment and was eating as much as he could, even against all medical advice.

For me to lose half my body weight, it would take quite a while to put it back on again—I couldn't do it in under ten weeks. With Ricky he was putting it on faster than he lost it in the first place.

I couldn't swear on the Bible that Ricky's story is true, but I couldn't deny it; it certainly could be legitimate. Starving yourself that quickly would be very uncomfortable; it's such a remote area and how he got there is just as much a mystery as him being found alive after so long.

Unless he was very familiar with the area, it would be a big risk to walk into the desert by choice even if he could create shelter. The only reason I can think of as to why he would do it on purpose is if he was trying to create a sensation by writing a bestselling book about being a 'survivor'.

Whatever his intent, he took a significant risk if he did it on purpose. It's an awful situation to put yourself in and, if you did it knowingly, you would be virtually committing suicide. Trying to starve yourself slowly and deliberately, you would have to be careful not to overload your digestive and metabolic system. It's one of the most horrendous ways to die you could imagine, with all your organs shutting down.

I first visited Dr David Welch about three weeks after Taz and Bruce found me. After a week or so I was out of hospital with no major ailments; I was in need of a medical check-up and picked out his Stuart Park surgery from the Darwin phone book.

As is clear from Dr Notaras's comments, the doctors at Darwin Hospital didn't really know what to make of me so I was glad to finally see someone who did. I had spent 71 days out there in the desert and lost 60 kilograms in the process, only to get into trouble for eating too much too soon.

Dr Welch was different. He wanted to know what foods kept me going out there and how I managed to survive for so long. By coincidence I learned he is not merely a doctor but a publisher, and that he published *17 Years Wandering Among the Aboriginals*, which is the true story of English sailor James Morrill, who spent seventeen years living with Aborigines in the mid-1800s in uncolonised north Queensland. Morrill was shipwrecked on a reef and floated for 42 days on a raft made from the mast before he managed to live off the land among the Aborigines.

Dr Welch knew that what I had done was possible in a good wet season if a person was prepared to do anything to make it, and he never doubted me. He has kindly provided me with the following commentary:

Ricky looked extremely emaciated when he first came in to see me, but better than the photos I saw in the newspaper. I was aware of his story from the media and, because of my interest in Aboriginal culture and desert survival, I was keen to hear what he had to say.

A lot of people have died in similar situations to those Ricky found himself in, but that's usually from a lack of water. You don't have to be out in remote bushland during that time of year very long for water to become a major problem. You can lose a few kilograms just going for a decent hike without it.

He was fortunate in being lost and stranded during a good wet season. Having water meant he wasn't going to die within days, but he still had to find food and try to get himself out of his predicament.

There are bush foods he could live on if he knew where to look, but most people wouldn't know about them. Things like small lizards, frogs and certain plants are edible, but some plants need preparation to make them less toxic to eat. There are often yams underground, for instance, but some need cooking to be palatable.

For someone with virtually no bush experience, I think Ricky did remarkably well. He soon worked out what was edible, and that food helped keep him alive. Aborigines lived in parts of the desert and semi-desert because they had built up a knowledge of foods, much more than anyone else, but this is quite different to someone suddenly landing in a remote bush environment and expecting to survive.

After treating Ricky and speaking with him I have no doubts he spent a long time in extreme circumstances. Knowing this I find it strange if some people are sceptical of his story. For a start, he lost a lot of weight and he also had a lot of swelling in both legs, consistent with being extremely malnourished.

When he first came in to the surgery, he was wearing compression bandages on both legs to reduce this swelling, which took several weeks to settle. Initially, my concern was whether this swelling was due to other serious conditions such as heart failure, liver failure or kidney failure; but, after examining him and getting more tests, I found these organs were okay. I told Ricky to take aspirin every day to prevent deep vein thrombosis from forming in his swollen legs.

Besides the swelling, Ricky was complaining of deep pain in a left tooth he had to break off himself when he was stuck out bush. He needed to see a dentist for his tooth. He also had a rash in the form of raised red rings scattered over much of his body. He thought he had suffered this in the past as a reaction to stress, but it proved to be a massive tinea (fungal) skin infection, worse than one usually sees because Ricky's immune system was low after suffering so terribly with malnutrition. The rash was so severe, it was difficult to treat and non-responsive at first, eventually clearing with a prolonged course of anti-fungal tablets.

I requested a series of blood tests to check on the oedema (swelling) and to make sure we weren't missing anything. Ricky's electrolytes (blood chemistry) were fine and so was his kidney function. Some of his liver enzymes were raised, consistent with his state of malnutrition, but I was not concerned.

Ricky told me that the hospital doctors had said his blood electrolytes should have been abnormal because of his malnutrition, and that this was inconsistent with his story of being lost. By my reckoning, his electrolytes may have been different in the last days that he was stranded out bush, but as soon as he had any further food and water, I wouldn't expect them to necessarily be abnormal. The body tries to maintain normal blood sugars and blood chemistry despite a state of starvation or thirst. We might lose a tremendous amount of our weight, but our blood chemistry is being maintained at normal levels so that our internal organs and brain can still function.

As for the way our body deals with malnutrition, first, as we go into a state of hunger, we are using carbohydrates stored as glycogen in our muscles and liver. The first energy source is glycogen. Once you have used up your glycogen stores, next the body uses the fat stores for energy, and your weight is reducing. Only with severe hunger, as faced by Ricky, do you then start to use your body proteins for energy. Protein is essentially your muscles, and that is when a person gets the muscle wasting that Ricky suffered.

Few Europeans since the early explorers have survived in such a barren part of the Australian bush, under such harsh conditions, as Ricky has done. In the past, it was only with the assistance of local Aboriginal groups. His tremendous weight loss tells that he was unable to find enough food to maintain an equilibrium.

It's good to see he is now back to looking normal. I couldn't understand why there was any great controversy about how quickly Ricky put his weight back on, as his body would tell him if he was eating too much—he would vomit or have diarrhoea if he couldn't handle it.

Ricky seems very robust and mentally strong and he's very lucky he had the good wit to think of eating whatever he could find. He had a good wet season and was prepared to eat bush foods, so he gave himself every opportunity to survive. If he didn't have those two things going for him, he would have died pretty quickly.

19

RETURN TO BOREE

A lot of people doubted my story, based on what they had read in the papers, and I can't really blame them. 'Mystery Man Survives Three Months Lost in Desert' was the first headline to herald my survival.

I saw the headline on the front page of the local Darwin newspaper while I was still recovering in hospital. It was accompanied by a photo of an unknown person with their face blacked out because they didn't have a picture of me. I wondered who they were talking about. All of a sudden I was a mystery man.

The article went on to tell the tale of an extremely emaciated man who 'is calling himself Ricky Megee' and had been found on a remote cattle station. They quoted a doctor from Darwin Hospital I'd never seen before and a station manager I'd met for all of twenty seconds when he'd stuck his head in to say hello in the hospital a few days earlier.

I'm not 'calling myself Ricky Megee'; I've been Ricky Megee for nearly 36 years, ever since my mum and dad named me that when I was born. These people know nothing about me or who I am.

The article also quoted Birrindudu station manager Mark Clifford as saying I told his workers that I'd experienced car problems on an isolated stretch of road and tried to walk to the homestead. He was quoted as saying that 'a lot of city people come up here and they're basically inexperienced and don't know what they're getting themselves into on these really isolated outback roads in a vehicle that's not equipped for it'.

I'm not sure where Mark had sourced his information from. But what was written in the newspaper certainly never came from me or anyone I'd spoken to about my ordeal.

He was certainly right about not knowing what I was getting myself into, though. I would never have picked getting drugged and left for dead in the desert. I'm not sure you can equip a vehicle for that.

Out of frustration I decided to give Mark an earful and called him up. I realise now it wasn't his fault and I consider Mark to be a very decent man; but at the time and in that state of mind I gave it to him over the phone for telling the press things that weren't true, things I've never said to anyone. The article had wrongly turned the whole thing back on me.

If I was going to get lost like that on my own, I'd at least like to think I'd have put my shoes on. Maybe even grab some of the water I had sitting in the Esky so I didn't have to drink my own piss. It was a pretty strange place to get my car bogged for no reason and I'd invite anyone who thinks I staged it all to grab some attention to spend 71 days walking on my shredded feet and see how they cope.

But people didn't want to hear this. Instead I had journalists pretending to be friends and trying to sneak into the hospital to get the inside scoop. And when I checked out of hospital they tracked me down to where I was staying.

I was living in a shared house which ironically I had found in the classifieds section of the 'Mystery Man' edition of the local paper about ten days after being rescued. But the people there asked me to leave within hours of my arrival because they were freaked out by all the media attention I was getting. I don't blame them—I was in the middle of a three-ringed circus, and guess who they wanted to feed to the lions.

Once I had changed SIM cards though, the phone stopped ringing from people I didn't want to speak to and I was able to move out to a rural area to get away from it all. I had a nice little house on a few acres where I could start to get my life back in order, find a job for money and motivation, and move on with my life.

As I put more weight on, people no longer recognised me as the bloke who'd been found starving in the desert. So much so that, if I had stood at the bar and told the guy next to me that I was that skeleton fella they'd plucked from the outback, he probably would've punched me in the face for being queer. Such is the honesty in Darwin.

The boredom of having nothing to do in a town where I knew virtually no one was grinding at me so the chance of a job as a guide taking tourists on four-wheel drive safaris through Kakadu and Litchfield national parks was not one I wanted to let pass me by.

It was good to be outdoors and the tourists enjoyed my company if my Guide of the Month award was anything to go by. But my strength wasn't returning as quickly as the kilos and the physical effort required became too demanding eventually. For the same reason I had to throw in my next job as a pool cleaner. And then my ankles started playing up.

In my five months since being found I'd been a tour guide, a pool cleaner, a carer for a disabled woman, a courier and a milkman. Some people don't have that many careers in their lifetime, but none of them were for me and so I returned to being a heavy-machinery operator.

I'm not sure what I was searching for in those first few months out of hospital but I knew I wouldn't be able to leave the Territory without returning to the station where it had all begun. Maybe that's part of the reason why I decided to stay in Darwin in the first place.

I didn't know anyone, didn't have a job and wasn't intending to come here before I was hijacked; but the weather was nice, the people were friendly enough and there was no point going to Port Hedland. I didn't want to go back home to Brisbane either, because of the temptation to slip into bad habits and hang around with the wrong crowd.

I knew I had to set eyes again on the dam where I had lived for seven awful weeks. To soak it up and say goodbye.

When Taz and Bruce had rescued me, it had all happened pretty fast. I barely had enough time to grab my tooth, car keys and my shredded shorts from the humpy as souvenirs, let alone to absorb my surroundings one last time. I also wanted to go back to where it all happened and capture as much as I could on film; to substantiate my story. Not that I need any reminding, but to provide reassurance to anyone who doubted me.

Just when I was getting ready to head back out to visit the dam and to shoot the documentary I had planned, I again ended up in hospital and under the surgeon's knife.

I had gone to see the doc about my right ankle, because there was fluid oozing out of it, and he sent me straight to hospital, where they diagnosed an infection. Because I'd lost all the muscle around my bones, the screws in the plates in my ankle from my previous accident had come loose and they were worried about the infection settling in.

I'd had this problem before, when they'd treated it successfully with drugs, but these guys seemed pretty keen to cut me open and have a good dig around just to be sure. To the surprise of everyone but me, they put me under anaesthetic and had complications with the surgery, leaving me with a pus-oozing wound that took weeks to heal properly. Meanwhile the doctors decided to treat the infection with drugs after all, guaranteeing me eight more days in hospital for no reason.

It was early July by the time I felt strong enough for any kind of trek, and Greg and I were ready to set out for the station.

I was living with Greg by this stage. We met when he came out to interview me after I first left hospital for the newspaper he worked for. At a time when no one really believed in me and I didn't know anyone, we'd forged a strong bond over the following months.

I could talk to Greg about how I felt and what I'd endured without feeling like a freak of nature—or a liar. The whole experience of what I'd survived had taken its toll and we determined to set out and prove exactly how incredible my journey was.

There were a few last-minute dramas, but we eventually hit the highway in the old Falcon I had bought off a friend of a friend for $1000, fully loaded with enough essentials to last us a good five days.

We had plenty of water, plenty of food, mozzie coils and insect spray; we were prepared for all eventualities.

Originally I had had visions of driving out there in a fully-decked-out four-wheel drive so we could follow the dry river bed all the way back to the windmill and then retrace my steps backwards and maybe find the tarpaulin I woke up under.

Because the country was now bone dry compared to six months earlier when I'd stumbled across the river in desperation, it would have been easy in a four-wheel drive to make my way back to the windmill. I knew I could find the route of the river easy enough using maps and taking notice of its proximity to other landmarks off the station road, but in the Falcon we didn't have the traction to follow the path. We could only work with what we had and we couldn't get our hands on a four-wheel drive, so the Falcon had to do.

We didn't warn the station manager, Mark Clifford, about our impending visit because we were afraid he would say no. The last time I'd exchanged words with him, things weren't very pleasant; documentary or no documentary, I wanted to go back out there and see where I almost died, even if it meant having to explain myself to him afterwards.

I had spent almost three months out there and virtually starved to death; I just hoped Mark would understand that when we appeared on his doorstep unannounced.

* * *

It's about 1100 kilometres to Birrindudu station from Darwin, with about a third of that on the dirt, depending on which way you go. We managed to add a couple of hundred extra kilometres on the dirt after missing a turn-off at Katherine.

The trip was pretty uneventful except for the usual kangaroos playing chicken with the car, including one big fella who was taller than the car even before he arced up at us. Driving into Kalkaringi felt pretty weird. While the locals sat around the petrol station eating chicken drumsticks, we stopped to make a phone call to the person we'd hired the camera off, to get a few last-minute instructions. They love their fried chicken drumsticks around here; they live on them.

Once we'd sorted the finer details on operating the camera, we were on our way on the final nervous leg of the trip to Birrindudu. The desert scrub ran past monotonously on either side of the road for the most part of the 180 kilometre stretch to the station and there wasn't much said between us as we came closer to our moment of truth. We were determined to reach the dam and had maps of the area from the Department of Lands, so knew roughly where we had to get to.

Ironically, where I was found isn't that far from Nongra Lake, a huge expanse of salt water in the middle of nowhere that covers a few station boundaries near the Northern Territory–West Australian border. According to the maps there was a road from the neighbouring station, Inverway, that accessed the lake and we decided that might be the best option.

I remembered Taz and Bruce telling me on the drive back to Birrindudu homestead that there was a track going right around the lake and I thought we could follow that from the neighbouring property and link up with the road to Boree, the remotest bore on the station. It sounded good in theory; the tracks were rock-hard when I was found and there didn't appear to have been much rain since then so I thought the Falcon should be able to handle the terrain.

As we puttered up the road to Inverway station, it became apparent we would have to drive right past its homestead, which is only a few kilometres from the turnoff. To do that, we'd have to talk to the guy driving the tractor behind the locked gates leading to the homestead.

As there was no avoiding that one, I wound down my window on the driver's side and caught his attention.

'G'day, mate, how are you? We were just passing through and had seen that big lake on the map with a road leading to it from here. We were wondering if we could go and have a look. I've heard it's a good spot to see migrating birds.'

He climbed down from the tractor and explained why we wouldn't be getting past his gates, bird migration or not. The road's a bog, he reckoned, you'd be flat out getting to the lake in a four-wheel drive from here and you're no chance in a Falcon.

Besides, he informed us, ever since that fella got lost out here a few months ago people around here have got a bit funny about letting people on the station. Of course, he had no idea he was talking to that fella.

I asked him if there was any other way to reach the lake and he pointed in the direction of Birrindudu. 'That's the only other road,' he said. 'You might be able to get down from there.'

I thanked him for his troubles and drove off again in the trusty Falcon. Turning the music up, I gave him a wave. *Fuck, fuck, fuck! We haven't come this far for nothing.*

All of a sudden I was back on that bloody road to Birrindudu, turning off the highway towards the big red gates that had given me so much hope when I came across them months earlier. If we had had a four-wheel drive we could've turned right and followed the track to the river and snaked back to the windmill. But without that option we paused at the big red gates to open them and continued on the road towards the homestead. The piles of cow shit and lack of bovines brought back memories of my desperate walk only a few months before.

About 50 kilometres down the Birrindudu road, I spotted the Boree intersection a few hundred metres in the distance. When I first reached the intersection six months earlier in search of salvation, it created confusion as I didn't know which direction to follow. Not to mention complete agony when I was bitten by a bush centipede. Not this time though—I knew to turn left towards Boree and find my dams.

But there was a problem. Not more than a couple of hundred metres past the intersection a four-wheel drive was parked; smoke was rising from a camp set up next to it just off the open road.

That would be right. There hadn't been a vehicle or the slightest hint of civilisation for 50 kilometres down this track until the one place where we didn't want them to be.

If these guys are station hands, we're fucked, I thought. We would have to go and see Mark and try and explain everything, and hope he showed me some sympathy. No matter if I turned down the track to Boree or kept going past our surprise campers towards the homestead, they were going to be scratching their heads about what an old Falcon was doing on the property.

With only a few seconds to decide what option to take, I kept on going—driving past them to get some indication of what they might have been doing there and to collect my thoughts. There were two blokes at the camp, enjoying a smoko, and they gave us a wary wave as we slowly drove past.

This is fucking stupid! We came out to find the track to Boree, and now I've just driven past it.

Angry and confused, I turned back towards the Boree intersection and pretended not to see the two campers. They didn't look like station hands, but they were obviously doing something on the property.

Now we were on the road to Boree, and I wasn't turning back for anyone. The road was a lot sandier than I'd remembered it and we'd gone not more than 500 metres when the tyres started to sink and slide.

It was those fine shiny black rocks bringing us undone, the ones Malcolm Douglas had shown me indicating water was underground. All the rain had well and truly seeped through the surface though, the baking sun transforming the tiny pebbles to a fine dust. I started to lose my steering; then the next second we'd gone too far and stopped completely.

We were bogged well and truly. I tried easing her out slowly and gunning it at full throttle, but half my back tyre was buried—the car wasn't going anywhere. *I can't believe this—twice! I'm fucking stuck again!*

I knew I'd have to swallow my pride and tell those blokes camped up the road who I was and what we were doing there, in the hope they could winch us out.

We walked back to the intersection filthy with ourselves, just as they were about to leave their camp. If they turned left towards the station now and didn't see us, we were fucked and would have to walk the 30 kilometres to the homestead to get help, which would take some explaining. Luckily though, they came our way and I flagged them down and told them we were bogged.

As it turned out they were a couple of locals who worked for the government and were doing a weeds survey on the property. Thank goodness for weeds!

When I first saw them I thought I was cursed, but they soon became a blessing. I wouldn't say they were delighted to see us, but they were happy enough to help us out and didn't ask for much of an explanation. They had a good chuckle when they saw the state of the track we had tried to drive the Falcon down though; then they drove off none the wiser.

Once we were out of the bog, there was no other option than to go and see Mark at the station and explain what we were doing there. I had intended to see him after we'd been back to the dam anyway, to explain what I'd been doing and why, and to give him back a bag of clothes Taz and Bruce lent me, which I'd been carrying around since discharging myself from hospital.

When I first talked to him after I'd been found, Mark had originally offered to get one of the boys to take me out to the dam in a four-wheel drive but I was pretty sure that offer would have been withdrawn once I'd abused him for speaking to the paper without getting his facts straight. I wasn't nervous pulling up at the homestead; it was something that just had to be done and I wanted to see them all again, anyway.

When I knocked on the door and Leigh answered, she didn't even recognise me. I was more than twice the size of the scrawny old man they'd pulled out of the desert and I sounded different as well.

'It's me, Leigh. Ricky. The guy you guys plucked from the desert. I've got some clothes for the boys.'

She was a bit hesitant to say too much and, after a brief chat, went in search of Mark.

Mark came across the lawn with a guitar case in his hand, looking every part the station manager with his broad-brimmed hat. Leigh pulled him aside to give him the news. I was expecting this day to come, he said, I just didn't think it would be so soon.

There were no hard feelings towards Mark from my side, once the dust had settled, and I apologised for what I said to him on the phone. It had just been hard to survive something so traumatic and then to have everyone doubt me when I was finally found.

I explained to Mark that I'd wanted to come out and see the dam where I almost died and to thank the boys personally for saving me. Nothing more. Mark appreciated my intentions, but made it clear the boys didn't want to see me because of rumours circulated around the station by the cops about the type of person I supposedly was.

'Everyone's a bit spooked, Rick,' Mark explained. 'The stories they're hearing about you and what happened. We're just simple country folk.' He told me he couldn't believe half the things he'd heard from the police and wouldn't pass judgement on me, but he couldn't speak for the others.

I had no idea what he was talking about and he didn't elaborate. It sounded like the cops had stitched me up good and proper in their discussions with the locals.

I told Mark about the book I wanted to write and that we were hoping to shoot some footage for a documentary as well. It's closure for everyone, I said. After this we can all walk away from it and move on with our lives.

Mark was good enough to say we were welcome to go out and have a look around for as long as we liked. He couldn't spare a four-wheel drive, but he reckoned the road was okay.

I couldn't really tell him that, no, actually the road is far from okay and the Falcon won't get much further than the intersection, because we just had to get winched out by a couple of weed surveyors. But it was good of him to give us permission—he could see it was just the two of us and we weren't out to cause any trouble for anyone.

What we were going to do now, I wasn't sure. It was early afternoon already and we had no chance of making the trek in the Ford Falcon. The only possible way to reach the dam, which from memory was at least 20 kilometres from the intersection, would be by foot. Not our first choice, but we were there now and we weren't going back to Darwin without seeing the dam.

Just to be sure we weren't being blocked by a small patch of sand, we walked up the track a few hundred metres past where we'd got bogged earlier. But, sure enough, there was no way the Falcon could make it.

The back of the car was full of food and camping gear. I calculated that if we could make it by late afternoon to the first dam, where I had spent eight or so days and which I guessed was about 10 or 12 kilometres up the track, we could camp in the humpy I'd built into the dam wall and walk to the second dam the next morning.

After packing food, water, blankets, cooking equipment and photographic and video cameras, we set off down the track to Boree.

20

A KIND OF CLOSURE

I couldn't believe I was walking down that fucking track again, only this time by choice.

The country was so much drier than before; there wasn't a hint of green grass to be seen and the track was a bog of fine sand in most places instead of being rock-hard and covered in mud.

We stopped at a ridge that exposed the sheer hopelessness of my situation those few months earlier, where the landscape stretched for 80 kilometres into the horizon with not the slightest sign of civilisation.

It was only July but it was hot. I could feel my ankles swelling up and my poor old mate Greg looked like a pack mule lumbering under all that gear on his back. My pack wasn't much lighter and we had to stop every kilometre or so for a drink and a rest.

We couldn't film a great deal as we slugged it out on the track because we were both too exhausted and weren't sure how much further there was to go. Each time we stopped, I had to go through the gruelling process of pulling my boots off, to give some temporary relief to my aching ankles.

I can't believe I'm doing this again! The right ankle was worse than the left at first, but then they alternated in thrusts of pain as I compensated for the sorest one while hobbling along the track.

Each rest made the next stint even harder because I started up again with cold feet and no energy. Greg looked done in as well and I didn't have the heart to tell him I didn't recognise this part of the track.

Because I had originally taken off through the scrub after the centipede bit me, I hadn't actually followed the track. I only found my way back to it by following the fence line.

I had walked through two fences in my centipede-induced delirium the first time around, but at that time I couldn't be sure whether they were from the same fence or they separated different paddocks. Either way, I now thought we should have reached one of them in the hours we'd been plugging along the track and my doubts were becoming stronger.

The shadows were getting longer, but finally we did make the first fence, buggered but with still enough in the tank to get us to the dam.

It was freaky being back out there again. I certainly hadn't planned to be walking in when we prepared for this trip, but I knew that's what I had to do once circumstances conspired against us.

I was already in survival mode the second time around. I'd been here once before and at least knew what to expect. *Don't think about it, just do it—that's the key.*

With the fence line behind us, I thought the track should soon begin to slope down the hill any minute and then we would be home free. We'd been walking for four hours already and had gulped more water than we had planned, but there wasn't much choice. The conditions were so debilitating.

I'm sure Greg thought we were lost. We'd definitely walked further than the 10 kilometres I'd told him it would take to reach the dam, but finally the road began to slope down the hill like I remembered.

We're on the home stretch now, brother—the dam is just around the corner! And sure enough—there it was, but it looked pretty empty.

It looked pretty empty because it was empty. Bone dry, to be exact, and no bopples filled the paddock.

My humpy up the side of the dam had been kicked in by either cows or station hands. On closer inspection, I saw it was half-filled with dirt and requiring some major renovations before we could sleep inside.

We'd made it just in time for sunset. After relaxing for a few minutes, I managed to pull out enough dirt from the inside cavity of my humpy to squeeze the pair of us in.

This was where I lived once. I couldn't believe it—I was shocked to see the miserable state of it all. I certainly never expected the area surrounding the dam to be so dry in such a short space of time—it was unbelievable. Everything had died since I was first stuck out here. I wouldn't have lasted a day if I had been dumped a few months later.

Our water rations were getting desperate already. After dinner we left enough for a good slurp each in the morning and a trickle to carry on the walk to the next dam. I thought that even if it was bone dry at the second dam as well, there was a bore there we could pump some water from so thirst wouldn't claim us.

My ankles were bad though from a solid day's trekking, and if they didn't improve overnight I wasn't sure what I'd do.

Stuck at the dam, and sleeping in a hole again—that's red-hot!

* * *

It wasn't too bad inside the humpy. We had a blanket underneath to soften the rocks and threw one over the hole on top and also smothered one each around us for warmth. As the humpy had been built into the dam wall, we were insulated from the freezing cold surface winds; no mozzies could get in to easily attack us and the chilled winter air was kept out of our little cocoon until well into the morning.

I had some pretty nasty nightmares throughout the night, of being stuck out there again. Lying on my back, I was trying to fend off the fear that I could hear sounds coming from the edge of the paddock. I felt sure someone was watching us.

The noises sounded like a group of Aborigines chanting for me, like they were coming towards us to find out what we were up to. I kept having to shake off the possibility that someone would grab me as I huddled inside helplessly; I tried to concentrate on getting some sleep, but the nightmares persisted. Of course there was no one haunting me except my own exhausted imagination.

But it was my ankles that worried me most the next morning. I'd gone over on them again the previous night, when I was climbing up and down the dam bank, and they'd swollen up like little rockmelons overnight. There was no way I could make it anywhere lugging a heavy backpack and I wasn't sure I could reach the bore at the second dam, which I guessed was another 5 or 6 kilometres down the track, on two busted feet. The walk back to the car was even further and we didn't have any water to carry me there, so I hobbled off towards the second dam with little choice in the matter.

Along the track between the first and second dams was where I had found some waterlilies last time, but there was no chance of such luck this time around.

It was a pretty slow old pace with plenty of stops wherever we could find shade. My ankles were getting worse from the wear and tear but I just had to handle the pain, again. I couldn't just sit down and sulk there in the middle of nowhere.

Finally, after a few hours of peering around each bend in the hope of getting to the next paddock, we reached the tree line leading to the big green mounds that signalled our destination.

I was almost as glad to see them this time as on the first occasion. It was actually a bit harder to spot them now—they were more like patchy dirt mounds without their previous lushness—but I knew I wouldn't miss identifying them in a thousand years.

The acres of bopples I had stumbled through a few months previously had evaporated completely, but nonetheless we staggered the half a dozen kilometres to the dam feeling rejuvenated.

Stumbling through the dried weeds and with only a few hundred metres to go before reaching the dam, I stepped into a big hole that was obscured by spiky grass. The air was filled with expletives during those last few steps. If there was any doubt I wouldn't be walking out, that last stumble took care of it—before this I could hardly manage a shuffle, but now there was no chance of me making the return 20-plus kilometre journey.

Greg went and filled up our empty water bottle at the bore as I surveyed what was left of my big green mounds.

Everything looked different. The overflow dams, which had been full when I first arrived, were now empty. The paddocks I remembered stacked with bopple bushes had now turned to dust. If it had been like this when I arrived the first time, I would've been fucked for sure, no matter how hard I tried to eke out an existence.

The main dam was nearly empty. It was putrid with algae, and I wouldn't have dipped my little finger into it, let alone swallowed its contents. There was no vegetation around it at all, which meant none of the little creatures you could eat to sustain yourself. The transformation was incredible.

My humpy was still strong though—just how I had left it, pretty much.

Still, Greg came back from the bore with a smile on his face and a full water bottle, which we decided he would have to take with him when he walked back to the car to get help from the homestead.

I couldn't believe I was stuck out in the desert again, but there was no other way around me getting out. The circumstances might be different, but the result remained the same. Only this time I knew it wouldn't be terminal.

We sat there for a while going over our plan. We weren't desperate; we had plenty of fresh water from the bore and knew exactly where we were, but I could hardly walk to the edge of the dam, let alone back to the car. So we had no other choice than for Greg to make the long walk back on his own and raise the alarm.

As we were sitting there finalising things, we heard a chopper take off. It seemed to be from the direction of the homestead. We listened intently as the sound of the chopper blades gradually edged towards us, and then it crawled into view just above the tree line on the horizon.

Just like when the chopper had flown straight over me a few days after I first reached the second dam, this pilot again seemed to skirt straight over us even though we were madly waving our arms.

At first we hadn't been sure whether we wanted to get the pilot's attention. I knew Greg would make it back to the car and getting stuck out there again was a bit embarrassing, but I couldn't avoid the fact we needed help of some kind and I thought the sooner the better. So I swallowed my pride.

It appeared as though the pilot didn't see us because he was concentrating on checking for cattle on the paddock boundaries. I sat on my humpy swearing and cursing his total blindness. No acknowledgement and no attempt to put the chopper down—what a fucker! We reverted to our original plan for Greg to walk back to the car.

I was sitting on my humpy watching Greg skipping halfway across the open paddock with his blue water bottle dangling from his arm when the chopper, which had since moved on to another part of the station, turned back and circled us.

My mate kept walking as the pilot put the chopper down next to the dam and Mark Clifford jumped clear of the rotor blades with a wry smile on his face. He said he thought we might find trouble after speaking to the boys the previous night, who told him there was no way an old Falcon could get anywhere up the track to Boree. The chopper pilot had spotted our car ditched at the intersection and then followed our path to the second dam, before turning back to the homestead to collect Mark.

I told him I'd done my ankle in and couldn't walk any further; I pointed to Greg walking across the paddock to get help. Mark told me to sit tight and he'd be back in a couple of hours with a four-wheel drive. Once again I couldn't thank him enough.

He flew over to Greg and told him to turn back and wait at the dam, much to his relief. I think Mark was impressed we'd managed to walk so far in the desert heat. We were obviously determined to reach the dam where I had almost died, and hopefully he appreciated that my intentions were pure.

My tin was still out there. I remembered that my stick, the one that had carried me all that distance, was still buried in the foundations of my humpy. The bits of my shorts that I had used as a hat and a shelf lining were stashed under my old bed of grass, which remained in place.

It wasn't a traumatic experience to return to the dam, but it did make me revisit those feelings of utter desperation I'd experienced the first time around. I wouldn't have liked to have spent another night out there, that's for sure, and I was relieved that Mark didn't take much longer than a couple of hours to return in his single-cab Land Cruiser ute, similar to the one Taz and Bruce were driving when they rescued me, and pick us up.

Leigh's husband, Greg, came out for the ride as well. My mate Greg and I piled into the back, delighted to be finally heading home. We stopped to collect the remnants of our camp from the first night and pulled up at the Falcon twenty minutes later, hungry but happy it was all over.

Mark was really good about it all. He realised this was the last time I'd be bothering him, and that I'm a man of my word and wouldn't be back.

After a steak sandwich we prepared on the bonnet of the Falcon, we did some filming at the intersection and the big red gates and hit the Buntine Highway for the twelve-hour journey back to Darwin just as the sun was setting.

* * *

Although I wasn't able to retrace my steps all the way back to where I was dumped, it felt rewarding to see my main humpies again and to smooth things over with Mark.

It was unfortunate we had had to be rescued, but that was something that couldn't be avoided really and there was no harm done. We took a right-hand turn out of the station feeling reassured that we'd mostly achieved what we set out to do.

But about two hours into the trip, as we glided down the Buntine Highway, out plans hit another obstacle—this time literally, in the shape of a hulking desert bull.

Prior to his intervention the old Falcon had done us proud. But it's hard to argue with half a tonne of angry beast.

We both spotted him from about a hundred metres out, just off to the left of the road with his head down facing us. As we approached, he looked up briefly before crazily bolting at a right angle across the road and right into our path.

I hit the anchors and swerved hard to the left. Then, just when we looked like avoiding a collision, the bull inexplicably stopped dead still in the middle of the road to take the full impact.

We took out his back legs with the front headlight and he rolled over the bonnet and windscreen, ending up spreadeagled a couple of hundred metres behind us. How he didn't land in our lap I don't know, but it all happened so quickly we weren't worried too much about what could have been. We were more concerned with our buckled headlights and the water pissing out of the radiator.

Neither of us thought for a second about the bull, but I guess he died a painful death for being so stupid. It was like he was trying to commit suicide and to take us with him.

The force of the impact pushed the radiator back into the fan, which was now rubbing against the plastic casing, which was squeezed up against the engine mount. We were in big trouble if we couldn't get the fan working to cool the radiator this far out from home and so far from anywhere. It was unbelievable bad luck—here we were, stuck on the Buntine Highway where my ordeal had begun all those months ago.

I was fresh out of ideas to fix the problem. We somehow had to tug the front of the car forward so as to create some room to bang the radiator and fan back into place.

A couple of countrymen on their way to Kalkaringi approached us in their beaten-up four-wheel drive. After we waved them down, they slowed down for long enough to inform us they didn't have a tow rope before they drove on without lingering.

Our only option was to use some lengths of rope I had in the back and attach the front of the car to a tree. The idea was to go full throttle in reverse and hope this unbuckled the front.

I tied all the ropes together and gave it heaps on the gas, and hoped for the best. Luckily we were anchored to a big solid tree and this manoeuvre worked well enough.

With about 3 metres of rope to work with, I managed to tie all the necessary dangly bits to the banged-up body and we puttered along the last stretch of the Buntine into Kalkaringi at about 60 kilometres per hour, stopping just the once to fill up the drained radiator.

I knew that what remained of my former belongings, which had been rescued from the back of my old ransacked car after it was located, were now at Kalkaringi police station. So I decided to drop in and pay them a visit. The station wasn't open, but I rang the after-hours bell and spoke to the constable, who was at home next door watching the footy.

I'm pretty sure the last person he expected to hear from at 8.30 pm on a Saturday night in July was Ricky Megee. He and his copper mate came out to see me, surprised and curious.

Once they'd established who I was and asked what I was doing there, they took a walk around our busted-up Falcon and had a bit of a chuckle to themselves at the damage the bull had done.

They couldn't help me out with releasing my stuff, they explained. It would take three hours to go through all the paperwork and they didn't want to waste their Saturday night on that, so I would have to come back in the morning and they'd see what they could do for me.

One of them then cracked a funny and suggested we camp in town that night. That car's not safe to drive at night, he reckoned—there were donkeys and cows all over the road further along and we'd be likely to kill someone, if not ourselves, if we attempted the trip.

I told them I wouldn't feel comfortable spending the night in Kalkaringi, for obvious reasons, and they suggested camping on the outskirts of town instead. With no obvious solution, I told them I'd be back in the morning. But neither Greg or I had any intention of doing that or hanging around the joint for another minute, so I inched the Falcon back onto the bitumen.

The radiator was developing more and more holes in it, caused by nicks from the spinning fan. This made our emergency stops to fill up with water more and more regular. I could sit on 80 kilometres per hour, no worries, but we weren't travelling much further than 30 kilometres at a time and our water supply was running low.

We found a creek that was flowing steadily and filled up the 32-litre Esky to the brim. This was enough to get us the next 200 kilometres to Top Springs Roadhouse, where we camped the night.

The next morning we filled up with petrol and water. We were determined to maintain our schedule, but we were still about 600 kilometres short of our destination.

About 40 kilometres up the road from the petrol station we stopped for the usual top-up of water, but this time the poor old girl didn't have anything left to give when I tried to start her engine up again. Our car was cooked and so were we, without a snatch rope to tow us into Katherine.

The Buntine's hardly a tourist route and, being a Sunday, we settled in for what we expected would be a long wait. Greg was going to hitch the first ride he could get back to Darwin and borrow another vehicle he could drive back. Meanwhile I would either wait for him or get a tow into the next town.

We were sitting on the boot for less than an hour when outback legend Bob McClellan pulled up in his shiny new Toyota four-wheel drive, which he'd driven all the way from Sydney's Rose Bay. We called Bob an outback legend because without him we could've spent days on the side of the road. Bob told us he was heading to Broome to meet his wife for a holiday after trekking around the countryside for three months, and would be more than happy to help out a couple of stranded fellow travellers.

He was good for a tow for the 140 kilometres or so distance to the Victoria Highway intersection, which was only about an hour out of Katherine. Our outback legend had never used his snatch rope before, so I gladly hooked us up and we were on our way.

The rope snapped a few times along the highway and we got chatting to Bob as I put us back together again, telling him in a series of short conversations what we were doing stuck on the side of the highway. He's a top bloke and thought it was pretty amazing that the person he'd stopped to help on the side of the road was the same one they'd found in the desert only four months earlier.

Being the legend that he is, Bob didn't stop at the Victoria Highway intersection; instead he drove us 100 kilometres in a direction opposite to where he was headed so as to help us out. I'll call the wife and explain what happened, he said—she'll understand.

And, after all he did for us, he wouldn't even let us buy him a beer in Katherine. He just made sure we were okay and turned the car back around to continue on his journey.

Greg then hitched the 300 kilometres back up to Darwin while I spent the night in the car in the public car park across from where all the blackfellas drink in the park next to the river.

I must have looked pretty funny sitting inside the car with the smoke pouring off the gas stove while I cooked dinner on the front seat. A couple of cars full of young kids burned through the car park circling me throughout the night; I had a machete under my seat just in case, but there was no need to pull it out for those punks and they carried on.

The cops came by as well to see what I was doing and I simply told them I'd broken down and wasn't going anywhere until my mate came back the next morning.

Greg arrived early the next morning and we were about to tie up the tow rope to his borrowed Holden Astra and take the Falcon to the wreckers to sell for a hundred bucks when one of the locals driving past on his way back to work stopped and asked what we were doing. After telling him we were off to the wreckers, he offered me $250 if we could wait a couple of hours while he rustled up the coin from his boss; so we did what any decent Aussie bloke would do and went to the pub to wait.

Sure enough, on our third schooner he arrived with the cash and we shook hands, glad to see the back end of Katherine.

I wasn't expecting to arrive back in Darwin minus my car, but them's the breaks. I wasn't expecting to get dumped in the desert and left to die either.

* * *

If my extraordinary experiences prove anything, they just go to show that it doesn't always pay to help people broken down on the side of the road. But all the same, sometimes it's quite nice to be on the receiving end of the kind-heartedness of strangers when you're stranded.

More importantly, I reckon my story demonstrates that you should never, ever give up; no matter how confronting the circumstances. I still don't know why I was dumped and left for dead, or who exactly was involved. They are mysteries that will probably always elude me and I try not to reflect on them too much. It's too upsetting to dwell on and pondering the unknown doesn't achieve anything.

The suspense of waiting for someone to come and rescue me almost killed me, but I'm glad it didn't. In the end, I just wanted to live.

I had plenty of opportunities to give up, but each time I found a way to hang on just long enough for someone to find me. Each time it tocked for me to die, my soul kicked in and I kept ticking.

But my efforts to survive against all odds, using whatever means were at my disposal, should be uplifting to others. I'm just a normal guy who was caught in the wrong place at the wrong time; I don't think I did anything special, I just did all that I could to stay alive.

What I lived through is probably more than most people will have to endure, but anyone can apply those same instincts

I relied on to problems confronting them. Always keep your mind active; don't be afraid to try something just because it might not work; never abandon faith in your fellow man.

Be thankful for the good things in your life just in case they're snatched from your grasp and be sure to tell those you care about how you feel. It's no good wasting your energy on angry thoughts, you're better off dealing with the situation and planning ahead. Being afraid doesn't get you anywhere.

As the old saying goes, whatever doesn't kill you can only make you stronger. Always remember that life is worth living and be prepared to fight for it with every ounce of your soul. You just never know what tomorrow might bring.

RICKY MEGEE'S DESERT MENU

Vegetables

Abelmoschus ficulneus (native rosella)—'bopples', the main type of vegetation Ricky lived on

Cyanotis sp. (succulent perennial)—'spriggie-spriggies', similar to beans

Portulaca sp. (wild radish roots)—a prominent weed

Ipomoea muelleri (morning glory)—'schnurples', purple flowers

Nymphaea violacea (waterlily)—tasted like a spriggie-spriggie ice-block

Alysicarpus vaginalis (buffalo clover)—a bean-like weed

Cucumis myriocarpus (prickly paddymelon)—prickly melons that grow on a vine

Meat

blue claw crabs
lizards
leeches
brown and green frogs
praying mantises
caterpillars
crickets

grasshoppers
march flies
ants
bugs
mosquitoes
wasps
cockroach (one attempt)